The Missional Transition

The Missional Transition

INSIGHTS INTO REACHING
NEW MINISTRY HORIZONS
FOR CHRISTIAN LEADERS

George Creamer DMin

Copyright © 2017 George Creamer DMin
All rights reserved. This book cannot be reproduced and disseminated in any form by any means without expressed consent by the author. It is understood that any copying from, or duplication of, this report will not be allowed without consent by the author.

ISBN: 0692853359
ISBN 13: 9780692853351

Dedication

This work is dedicated to all Bible Institute students, past and present, from whom I have had the privilege to learn from and teach. I am forever changed by their honest desire to serve the Lord with their whole hearts. I am grateful for their friendship, sacrifice, and solidarity.

Contents

Introduction: The Transition toward Missional · · · · · · · · · · · · · · · · · · xi

Transition One: From Inward to Outward Focus · · · · · · · · · · · · · · · 1
Chapter 1   The Attractional Model · 3
Chapter 2   The Missional Model · 24

Transition Two: From Rigid to Flexible Space · · · · · · · · · · · · · · · · 49
Chapter 3   The Central Worship Site · 51
Chapter 4   Rethinking Sacred Space · 77

Transition Three: From Clergy-Led to Laity-Led Ministry · · · · 105
Chapter 5   Bridging Ministry Roles · 107
Chapter 6   Ministry Beyond the Building · · · · · · · · · · · · · · · · · 126

Transition Four: From Compartmentalized to Integrated Life · · 151
Chapter 7   Integrating the Sacred and Secular · · · · · · · · · · · · · · 153
Chapter 8   Faith and Vocation · 175

Last Things: · 207
Bibliography · 219

List of Tables and Figures

Table 1. Attractional Versus Missional Model · 28
Figure 1. Integrating Faith and Life to Avoid Compartmentalization · · · 165
Figure 2. John Holland's Hexagon · 190
Table 2. Post-Course Follow-up Responses · 193

INTRODUCTION
The Transition toward Missional

I WAS INTRODUCED TO THE term "missional" during graduate studies where I became intrigued by the word and spent several years pursuing its meaning. I wanted to learn as much as I could about how to become "missional" and how I could apply the concept in my own life and ministry. I set out on a pursuit to discover and become a "missional leader." Throughout the process, I attempted to apply my own research and study in practical ways in the various ministry roles in which I was involved. I am certainly not claiming to have attained all knowledge available on this topic. Far from it. But, I do feel the insights and valuable lessons I have picked up along the way can challenge readers to discover and apprehend new missional horizons.

The road has not been easy, and I have had my fair share of difficulties as I sought to serve the Lord faithfully. I have always wanted to be a resource to others, especially those seeking to increase their missional impact. Now, I can hand to those seeking to transition toward missional, a book filled with my most sincere reflections up to this point in life, as an educator and practitioner in Christian leadership. My intent is to provide key transitions that I see as critical to growth in missional capacity. Simultaneously, the book deconstructs debilitating mental models that have the potential to block Christian leaders from experiencing new ministry horizons. A brief overview of these transitions is found below.

THE TRANSITIONS: A BRIEF OVERVIEW

I have come to use the term "transitions" to explain how my thinking has expanded out away from the typical church paradigms. In this book, I develop four transitions that Christian leaders should consider adopting to begin thinking and acting more missionally. I prefer the word "pursuit" to describe my development, acknowledging that even though I have learned so much, I have not arrived and am still growing.

The **first transition** involves moving Christian leaders from an attractional leadership style toward a missional leadership style. The attractional church is explained as a model of ministry that focuses inwardly rather than outwardly. The inward focus can distract the church to the degree that the broader mission of God in the world is neglected. In contrast to the attractional mode, "the missional church takes seriously the call to 'go' and make disciples,"[1] outside of the confines of the church building. Mission is not only another program but the very DNA of why the church exists. Instead of the resources flowing primarily inward, the resources flow outward. The missional model promotes the idea that the church is not to be self-serving but is tasked with participating in the broader mission of God in the public sphere.

The **second transition** involves a different way of thinking about the use of sacred space. The church has seemed to be stuck in rigid patterns in terms of the usage of sacred space, which has kept it from thinking about more flexible, creative solutions. Traditionally, the church has thought of sacred space as an officially sanctioned building with a large cross and a church sign out front advertising worship times and the next event. In the sanctuary, there are seats in rows facing the stage and the pulpit, from which the pastor preaches. Contemporary churches have a worship group playing behind the pulpit with lyrics projected on the wall. The objective of this section is to begin to rethink about the meaning of sacred space away from this one-size-fits-all form of worship to more flexible, efficient, and organic possibilities.

---

1. Lee Beach, *The Church in Exile: Living in Hope After Christendom* (Downers Grove: InterVarsity Press, 2015), 2963, Kindle.

The **third transition** involves helping ordinary believers comprehend their part in God's redemptive plan in a post-church era. Shifting from clergy-led to laity-led ministry places ordinary believers in the driver's seat of the purposes and plans of God in their lives. Empowering ordinary members to develop a missional impetus can be difficult in some denominational circles since a culture persists—which started in the early centuries—that still categorizes Christians into two groups, the clergy and laity. The clergy are those called into ministry, while the laity are the ordinary and untrained believers, tasked with supporting the professional ministers in their churches. These stubborn mental models reinforce the divide between clergy and laity and hinder the whole people of God by creating two distinct groups of people, one more spiritual or endowed than the other. Clergy are tasked with most of the spiritual functions, while the laity serve the objectives of the clergy. This bifurcation unintentionally casts the laity as second-class in comparison to the professional, sanctioned ministers. This book promotes the concept that the reign of God can be just as tangible and accessible to the ordinary believer as the professional, full-time minster.

The **fourth transition** involves bridging the divide between the sacred and secular compartments of life. The concept that some activities are considered spiritual and others are considered secular is perpetuating the fragmentation that many believers experience in life. For Christians, all of life is sacred and there should be no separation. Who believers are at church—sons and daughters of the living God—should be the same identity they possess the rest of the week. When the church can begin to close the gap between the secular and sacred compartments it will achieve greater integrity. Living with greater integrity requires the surrender of all realms of life to the Lordship of Christ, including work, home, community, and recreation. When the church can close the gap between the sacred and secular, it will be more effective in impacting society in normal, day-to-day activities. The laity will see the hardest-to-reach places as their mission field. Particularly in the workplace, this has been a domain that has been a means to an end, as a paycheck. With a renewed vision, work can be a place that the Lord utilizes to advance his kingdom. After all, work is where most people spend the bulk of their time and where they already have significant influence.

Following the "Closing Thoughts" section of each chapter is a "Biblical Insights" section, which provides deeper biblical and theological reflection and serves as inspiration and springboard for the chapter's content. Then, the "Words and Phrases to Remember" sections define the salient terms in each chapter. "Scriptures to Reflect" lists verses from the Bible that may serve as starting points to enhance devotional time. Finally, the "Discovery Questions" give readers an opportunity to apply the material in a personal way.

TRANSITION ONE

From Inward to Outward Focus

THE FIRST TRANSITION INVOLVES MOVING Christian leaders from an attractional leadership style toward a missional leadership style.

CHAPTER 1

The Attractional Model

THE ISOLATING EFFECT

JOHN ONCE EXPLAINED TO ME that his concept of "church" was formed after his best friend, Leonard, became a Christian. After being saved, Leonard was on "fire" and started attending church regularly. What transpired in the weeks and months after Leonard's conversion was that he was no longer available to John because he was now consumed with all the activities and commitments expected of him as a member of the church. Missional author Reggie McNeal describes this experience from John's perspective as Leonard being "abducted by aliens" and "now living in the mother ship,"[2] referring to the isolating effect of his church involvement. Normally, they would spend weekends together having fun with their families. They would spend their summers playing golf, going to the lake, and taking family road trips. Ever since he started attending church regularly, however, Leonard was no longer available, and John felt shunned by his good friend. Leonard had become committed to his church and volunteered several times a week with hardly any time for recreation with John or anyone else from their circle of friends.

When they ran into each other during the week, Leonard always invited John to church. John then felt that any association with Leonard would mean participating with him in his church activities, if he wanted to spend any time with his good friend. Slowly, their friendship fizzled, and before long they rarely spoke to one another because John was not

---
2. Reggie McNeal, *Missional Communities: The Rise of the Post-Congregational Church* (San Francisco: Jossey-Bass, 2011), 11.

ready to make the same commitment to the church as Leonard. Leonard was now fully committed to the church's agenda, and his life revolved around its programs and activities. He wanted to make sure his fellow church members regarded him as a committed follower of Jesus, as he did not want his devotion to the church to be questioned. Leonard felt that if he was not present at most of the weekly functions, he would be considered a marginal Christian and remain on the fringes of his church community. He perceived that growing in Christ meant further involvement in church-related activities.

Since most of Leonard's free time was absorbed by involvement in the church's activities, he felt that inviting John to church was the best he could do to stay connected to his old friend. His friendship with John was reduced to attempting to talk him into going to church. As long as he remained committed and attended church, he was embraced and felt included by his fellow members. For him, going to church was a sacred practice, and anything outside of the limits of the church was secular. Service to the Lord meant volunteering in multiple activities. His involvement caused him to become increasingly isolated from the other areas of his life. His relationships within his circle of influence, which included extended family, work colleagues, and neighbors, suffered.

The attractional church model can potentially cause an isolating effect from those one is able to influence and lead to Christ. Also, John perceived himself to be Leonard's project to be won over and then to be showed off as a trophy at the next church service.

Leonard's story illustrates how effectively life can be separated into two compartments. The church grounds become the center for religious life and connection to spiritual practices. Life outside of the confines of the church becomes only a distraction from the truly spiritual matters within the church grounds. With this dualistic view of life, any outreach to the community seeks to draw people away from the unspiritual realm and into the spiritual zone. Attempting to extract non-members from their communities creates two realms or zones in the lives of individuals—sacred and secular.

THE ATTRACTIONAL MINDSET

Frost and Hirsch define an attractional mindset as "the practice of the Christendom-era of converting unbelievers, then extracting them from their cultural setting to join the church, thereby making them ineffective as missionaries to their own people groups."[3] Extracting individuals from their communities and absorbing them into the church culture can isolate people, particularly where they live and work. The practice of extracting individuals from their communities also causes believers with this mindset to cut themselves off from the people they can influence with their lives and the gospel message. This was the case with Leonard who cut himself off from his good friend, John. When the energy of the church is directed inward, it adopts a posture that Beach describes as "centripetal."[4] Outsiders are extracted from their spheres of influence when they join the church and are expected to acquiesce to the church's agenda, which is filled with programs, events, services, and other activities, which consumes all of their time and energy. No longer is there much time or energy left for family, friends, and acquaintances from their communities.

Additionally, an attractional posture tends to create a dualistic existence where members compartmentalize their lives between the secular and sacred. Spiritual matters are practiced in the religious zone, which is church property, while the secular realm is designated to everything that happens outside the church's turf. The problem is that the "secular turf" includes the neighborhoods and workplaces where most members spend the bulk of their time. The attractional mindset has a way of creating a bifurcated world by promoting the idea that what happens on church grounds is inherently more spiritual than the impact indigenous leaders can have in their own communities. In a time where the church is increasingly losing influence in the public domain, it is necessary that the church equips its members to engage their communities with their lives and the gospel, which will allow them to have impact where they spend most of their time and with whom they have developed meaningful relationships.

---

3. Michael Frost and Alan Hirsch, *The Shaping of Things to Come: Innovation and Mission for the 21st-Century Church* (Peabody, MA: Hendrickson, 2003), 228.
4. Beach, *The Church in Exile*, 2904, Kindle.

The rapport that individuals develop with neighbors and coworkers opens the door to sharing faith in a more natural fashion. Church members then see the ministry potential right in front of them in the places where they live and work. The church needs trained leaders who seek to dismantle the idea that God is not interested in all of life and that there is no need to label some practices religious and others unreligious.

Come-to-Us

Missional scholars Michael Frost and Alan Hirsch define attractionalism as:

> An approach to Christian mission in which the church develops programs, meetings, services, or other "products" in order to attract unbelievers into the influence of the Christian community. While there is an element to which the New Testament church was attractive and enjoyed the favor of the broader community (in some contexts), we believe that the contemporary church now almost totally relies on an attractional approach to its community.[5]

The attractional model of church is a "come to us" posture of ministry where outsiders are expected to voluntarily seek out the worship center of their own volition to find spiritual nourishment. In this model, the energy is directed inward and its mission is to draw people in. This church seeks to draw "outsiders" to attend one of its scheduled services by attracting them. This model worked in a society with a built-in disposition to seek out the church. It worked in a society where going to church was embedded in the fabric of the culture and during an era when the U.S. was considered a predominantly Christian nation.

During this time, one of the characteristics for being a good American was going to church on Sunday. It was expected that coworkers and neighbors would also share the same Christian beliefs. In the past, most of American society had some knowledge of the major biblical themes.

---

5. Frost and Hirsch, *The Shaping of Things to Come*, 226.

During this era, referred to as "Christendom" by missional authors, with all the various denominations competing for worshipers on Sunday, there was a pressure from church leadership to try to lure outsiders into their building. This strategy focuses on being "attractive" to non-members by getting the internal programs right, having a beautiful building, installing state-of-the-art stage lighting and audio-visual systems, hiring talented worship leaders, charismatic preachers, and so on. There is a belief that these features will irresistibly pull "outsiders" inside the church doors.

For missional scholars Frost and Hirsch, the fact that the church building continues to be designated as the place of worship makes it "more static and, as a consequence, almost exclusively attractional. The primitive church in the first century had no recognized dedicated buildings other than houses and public spaces."[6] Frost states, "It is an assumption that locates the central purpose of the Christian community in the act of corporate worship."[7] Corporate worship is an integral component of the body, but it should not be the only or the central focal point of the church. This is especially detrimental to the impact the church can have on the broader culture, when a focus on gathering causes the body of Christ to neglect its missionary duty and the ongoing mission of God in their communities. The focus on corporate gatherings as the thrust of Christian worship tends to isolate the faith community with little or no connection to the surrounding neighborhoods.

INDIVIDUALIZED SPIRITUALITY

Attaching God's presence to a physical location can cause an individualized spirituality where church becomes a place to acquire religious goods and services and the minister serves as the vendor. Faith becomes individualized when the purpose of going to church is to be served by professional ministers. The congregants' role is to pay for these services through their tithes and offerings. This also maintains the ancient division between clergy and laity. Congregants go to church to be fulfilled spiritually and to

---

6. Frost and Hirsch, *The Shaping of Things to Come*, 226.
7. Michael Frost, *Exiles: Living Missionally in a Post-Christian Culture* (Peabody, MA: Hendrickson, 2006), 277.

be ministered to by the professional ministers. There are no implications of what it means to be God's people in the grand scheme of his redemptive plan for the world. This mentality will render the church powerless and irrelevant if it cannot see beyond its spiritual bubble.

This individualized Christianity is detrimental to spiritual growth because faith is about having personal needs met. When faith becomes individualized without making a connection with the broader mission of God for the world, "Elements of the worship service, including the preaching of the Word and the worship of God, become reduced to a form of therapy that places the individual at the center of the worship service."[8] The church becomes fixated on its programs as the means to meet the individual needs of its people. The church becomes compelled to keep its clientele happy, so they are always looking for new products and services they can promote to keep congregants engaged and spiritually filled. This individualized spirituality causes people to compartmentalize their lives between the sacred and secular areas of life. Sunday church becomes a place to have spiritual needs met without any implications for the rest of the week in the other realms of life.

Self-Focused

With the church building and corporate worship at the center of spiritual life, evangelism is about getting people to attend and participate in church activities. Any outreach beyond the church walls has the explicit purpose of getting outsiders into the religious zone. In this posture, the church becomes distracted with its churchly affairs, which sidelines God's mission in the communities where they are located. With the focus tuned to its internal management, the church becomes blind to its surroundings and cannot respond to the call of God to impact neighborhoods. Missional author Reggie McNeal writes, "We've spent so much time in the attractional church trying to get the community to connect to us; now we need

---

8. Soong-Chan Rah, *The Next Evangelicalism: Freeing the Church from Western Cultural Captivity* (Downers Grove: Intervarsity, 2009), 309, Kindle.

to learn how to connect to the community."⁹ The attractional church expects outsiders to acquiesce to its agenda and programming instead of relinquishing its plans for the sake of others.

In contemporary culture, a self-focused posture is termed "attractional" by Frost and Hirsch, a mindset which claims, "If we get our seating, our parking, our children's program, our preaching, and our music right, they will come."¹⁰ This is not to say that the church should not be attractional, but when its focus is exclusively inward, Jesus's vision for the church to go to the ends of the earth with the gospel message and make disciples will be hindered. The attractional model causes the location of the church to become the center of religious life, and any outreach to the community seeks to draw people into their building. Essentially, the church becomes set on motivating individuals to leave their turf and join the church's turf. When the energy is inwardly focused, however, it causes the church to become self-absorbed and consumed with meeting and maintaining its internal needs (buildings, budget, and attendance). There is also a strong pull to try to get people across into the religious zone because they are the ones who will provide the resources the church needs to stay afloat. In the attractional church, the energy is directed inward and seeks to get people to "come and stay." Rather than the priority being the church meeting the people's needs, the people now meet the church's needs and hopefully theirs will be met in the process.

Double Standard

One of my relatives consistently asks me to visit her and her family in another state. Occasionally, she will send a text or make a comment on Facebook that my wife and I should visit her. I have visited several times in the past, and we always have a great time. She comments on their beach house and the activities she has planned if we were to visit. She talks about the new toys they have acquired; for example, they recently bought a new jet ski. They post pictures on Facebook showing the world how much fun

---

9. Reggie McNeal, *Missional Renaissance: Changing the Scorecard of the Church* (San Francisco: Jossey-Bass, 2009), 53.
10. Frost and Hirsch, *The Shaping of Things to Come*, 19.

they are having at their beach house. She always uses the beach house to entice me to visit her.

I must confess that my desire to visit her has dwindled significantly in recent years, mainly because she has been in my city on more than one occasion and has yet to stop by to visit me. As it happened, not long ago, she was driving cross country. She drove through my city, posted some pictures of the sights on Facebook, with no intention of stopping by to say hello. Naturally, this rubbed me the wrong way because I felt I needed to take the initiative and take a flight out to see her even when she was in town. This was not the first time she had passed through without stopping by.

I tell this story only to illustrate the mindset of an attractional church. There is a double standard. The church invites and tries to attract people to them in a "come to us" posture. They expect others to take the initiative, but they do not reciprocate and "go to them." It becomes a singular focused relationship where there is a lot of take but little give. Especially in an era where the church is losing influence, this posture is no longer feasible if the unchurched are to be won for Christ. The church cannot sit back and expect folks in the community to relinquish their plans to the church's agenda. The church needs to be taking the first step without expecting anything in return. Church members need to visit the people they are hoping to reach in the communities, on their turf, if they expect them to reciprocate.

The Building is the Glue

My mom and I attended the same church at one point. After a few months, she stopped going because she was afraid to drive on the busy freeways in Houston. I was unable to pick her up because I had some obligations on the other side of town, so I would drive straight to service. When I started showing up without my mom, it was natural that members would ask me about her and how she was doing. After several weeks, some were still asking me about her whereabouts. I began to get frustrated with the same question over and over. I thought, "You ask me about her every time I see you, why haven't you tried calling her and ask her yourself how she's doing?" I think the attractional pull causes members to have this type of predisposition toward others. In an attractional church, fellowship tends to revolve around the church premises. The church building becomes the glue that keeps people connected to one another, but it typically does not extend outside the physical location. My mom's association with the church was based on her ability to get to church.

She confessed to me later that she felt no real connection with anyone at church and her relationships felt relatively artificial. She felt her connection was conditional. When she could make it onto church grounds, she felt included and embraced. Otherwise, she remained on the fringes, and relationships could not be nurtured unless she had attended service where "true" fellowship could take place. Her connection with the people was commensurate with her ability to attend the scheduled church services. The church did not realize that someone stopping by and taking her out for coffee might have had a greater impact on her than a Bible study or sermon.

RETENTION

Any good car salesman knows that the objective is not to let the customer leave the lot. If they do, even though they promise to come back and buy, the car salesman knows they have lost the sale forever. Therefore, car dealerships make it as difficult as possible for people to leave by luring them with rewards and benefits. They have become creative, offering food, childcare, and entertainment to keep customers from leaving. They know that there are multiple lots down the road that are going to work hard to earn that business. Churches use similar strategies to prevent people from going down the street to the next church. There is a preoccupation with getting people to "stay" and to make them feel comfortable, instead of equipping individuals to "go" and live missionally in their neighborhoods and workplaces. The attractional model seeks to provide products and services that will persuade them to stay. There is an expectation for members to sell the church to customers, to impress them enough so they will come back instead of going to their competitors.

Some churches have opened schools, gyms, bookstores, day care centers, and cafes to draw people. Some of the larger attractional churches have created a "mall effect." Spiritual shoppers do not have to leave the church premises (or do not want to) because everything they need is inside. The church offers attractive elements to draw people into the church so that they can feel at home, making them want to stay. Even social life can be confined to associating with other members of the church. Making friends outside of church feels unnecessary when churchgoers have an abundance of prospects that have similar beliefs and lifestyles.

The attractional church seeks first to fund its own efforts and projects. An attractional church may build a gym or elementary school on the premises without thinking about the parks and schools within the community that could use their help. Restoring the town's basketball courts or encouraging mentors to volunteer in the school's after-school programs does not guarantee new church members. The attractional church may take on a competitive approach—to build something better than what the community offers, so that people will come to the church for quality programs.

An attractional church may host a Fall Festival event, competing with the events within the community with better games and attractions, to take people away from the community's yearly festival. Instead, the church could partner with the community and find out how they could help provide a better festival than the previous year without any strings attached. When the church seeks to put others first, it takes away the competitive side in ministry. It also takes away the pressure to try to win over individuals by beating out the competition. Relationships are easier to nourish when congregants are looking out for the needs of the community. If individuals decide to join the church, it is because there was an effort to build bridges with community and not because the church offered better amenities.

Cruise Ship Mentality

The absorption on the internal programs reminds me of the experience I had when my wife and I went on our first cruise. This experience made me think of the attractional model. As we waited to board the ship, vast amounts of food, water, and supplies were being loaded onto the ship.

Pallet after pallet of resources for the trip restocked the now empty ship. Once passengers were on board and the ship set sail, the crew and ship provided everything vacationers could possibly want and need. The goal was to make the experience as memorable as possible, providing exceptional service and entertainment with the hope that passengers will look forward to coming back for their next vacation. The passengers were provided a menu of options for the day from which to pick. There were events and programs for everyone in the family. I was amazed to see all the various activities that were available every day. The crew kept all the passengers busy with activities; rooms were cleaned; meals were prepared; schedules were organized; passengers were free to just be.

BUILDING, BUTTS, AND BUDGET

> A 2014 study issued by the *Evangelical Christian Credit Union* broke down how our churches are spending their money. On average, they dedicate 58% to personnel expenses, 18% to facilities and maintenance, 6% to administration and 3% to cash reserves, paying off debt and to building funds. This leaves 14% for "Programs," which includes 5% for child and adult education, 2% for worship and 3% for evangelism/outreach (advertising, recruitment and P.R.). If you're tracking so far, this leaves 3%, 2% of which goes to overseas charities, and 1% of which is given to local and national causes outside the building. And though it can be argued that the programs inside church buildings do benefit both those who attend the church and sometimes those in the surrounding community, the fact remains that only $3 out of every $100 we give to our churches leaves the building. In short: when we are given a large pool of resources, we share less of it with people we're not personally connected with [inside the Church] than [with] those outside of the Church.[11]

---

11. Christian Piatt, "Does Religion Make Our Kids and Us Jerks," *Patheos*, November 17, 2015, accessed March 16, 2016, http://www.patheos.com/blogs/christianpiatt/2015/11/does-religion-make-our-kids-and-us-jerks/.

In an attractional model, the energy of the church is primarily focused on the matters that affect the internal functioning of the congregation. Running and operating the programs and services of the church consume the bulk of its resources. Activities, services, and meetings take up most of schedule of the congregation and it becomes a self-serving entity. The pressing issues are related with inward concerns: the building, attendance, budget, programs, staffing, and bulletins. An easy way to remember this concept is by the phrase "the three Bs: building, butts, and budget." Making sure that people come to the service is important because the individuals attending the services are the ones who tithe, volunteer, and provide financial backing so the ship continues to stay afloat.

As attendance increases, additional funding is needed to accommodate the growth which requires more expansion. The cycle continues, creating a massive machine that needs to be fed with extensive resources to continue operating properly. The first instinct of numerical growth is to build bigger facilities to accommodate the increase, which then requires additional resources to meet the expenses associated with physical expansion. This creates a pressure for the church to continue filling its pews to keep the machine running. Its priorities revolve around the concerns of its members, which eats up most of its resources because of the vast expenses required to keep members involved and absorbed in the life of the church. The church's life becomes absorbed with events and activities that keep congregants busy and engaged. The church is too busy with its own agenda to think about or do anything else that does not involve its own interests.

Board members are consumed with addressing the issues concerning the inward needs of the church. Any talk about missions usually involves allotting a fraction of the budget to send to overseas missionaries so they can feel they are doing their part in spreading the gospel. Spending on outward-focused initiatives boils down to sending denominational headquarters their cut of the budget to keep the authorities happy. An attractional church, in Kennon L. Callahan's words, "focuses more on membership than on salvation, more on institutional maintenance than on societal outreach, more on the concerns for lost dollars of giving than on mission with specific human hurts and hopes."[12]

Focus on Activities and Programs

Most of the time in meetings is absorbed by internal logistics and funding so that all activities and programs will continue to run smoothly. The church needs to remain attractive, so it will continue to motivate people to get up on Sunday morning. In the attractional model, the glue is the building itself where there is a dependency on the location for relationships and service. This model expects outsiders to leave their comfort zones and infiltrate religious turf. Instead of meeting people where they are on their terms, the attractional church expects the unchurched to become enculturated by the churched culture. Relationship building with outsiders can be disingenuous because the end goal is inviting them to church. The congregants are tasked with bringing people from their spheres of influence so that the professional pastors can minister to their needs. Upon arrival, they will be offered a menu of programs and services from which to choose. Also, this is the congregation's opportunity to shine and show their hospitality during the time before and after service. Discipleship becomes no more than attending one of the scheduled Bible studies available at the church. Church life revolves around the activities and events of the church as if God's presence were localized to a place.

Membership

> The attractional model of church creates a "member culture," in which people join a particular church and support that organization with their attendance, their money, their prayers, and their talent. The flow is toward the church, which is always at the center of the action, where the big game is being played.[13]

---

12. Kennon L. Callahan, *Effective Church Leadership: Building on the Twelve Keys* (San Francisco: Jossey-Bass, 1990), 26.
13. Reggie McNeal. *Missional Communities: The Rise of the Post-Congregational Church* (San Francisco: Jossey-Bass, 2011), 54.

A characteristic of an attractional church is its overt concern with membership as a key element for sustaining the church. There is no question that there are benefits to membership. While a sense of commitment, accountability, and responsibility to the local church are valuable principles to instill in congregants, there are also some drawbacks to membership. Members are usually required to be fully committed to attendance, tithing, and volunteering within the church. This has the potential of further isolating them from their surrounding culture because there is now an expectation for them to be even more committed to the functioning of the church. Churches that are membership-driven can place high expectations on their members, placing pressure on them to be involved in the various activities and programs lest they lose their status. They are sometimes asked to sign a document stipulating the requirements that need to be maintained to be in good standing as an official member. These requirements place an emphasis on the internal needs of the church, which takes away from other spheres of influence where they can have Kingdom impact, including their workplaces and communities. The two-part word "member-ship" says it all. Attractional churches look to reward commitment by making faithful "members" an integral part of the "ship."

In a recent visit to a congregation that prided itself in being missional, it was obvious that it was program- and membership-centered and that missions was one program among many. This congregation had a "Pathway of Leadership" in place with a list of requirements for those who were pursuing greater responsibility within the body. The first step was to sign a document promising to adhere to membership stipulations, which included regular attendance on Sunday mornings and tithing ten percent of income. Additionally, candidates had to become regular attenders of a small group and complete six foundational classes. Their premise of membership was that it was biblical, the document referred to 1 Corinthians 12. Additionally, the document stated that "true membership is indicated by participation." Status of membership was heavily reliant on involvement and commitment to the plethora of activities and programs offered by the church. The last statement on the document read, "You can still come to church if not a member. Everyone is welcome." The notion is that non-members will be tolerated but will not feel included. This process creates a culture that requires one to become absorbed by the internal programs to avoid remaining an outsider.

This congregation's membership process has the potential of making some worshipers feel inferior spiritually. If Christians feel like outsiders, it should not be in the church but in the world as they seek to live faithfully. In an attractional model, unless worshipers adhere to the church's agenda and requirements, they will not feel fully accepted into the body. In this context, individuals cannot serve unless they have gone through the membership process, which elevates them to a step above the average attendee. There is a culture where promotion to member status is based on the level of commitment to the goals and objectives of the church. Sometimes maturity is equated with membership when the reality is that it is only a commitment to the church's agenda. Membership is equivalent to an individual's commitment to Christ. If members are involved in activities and programs, they are growing and on a discipleship path. Service to God is equated with one's level of involvement in church-related activities. Any service outside of the church location becomes inferior or less spiritual and often is not even recognized. Church leaders are careful not to "push" member involvement in outreaches and ministries that will not benefit their numbers

COMPARTMENTALIZATION

The attractional model of worship developed from Christendom is a style that is still functioning today where the church perceives it is still at the center of culture. A congregation that finds itself on the "high" side of attractionalism is overtly absorbed with its own agenda to the extent that it gradually becomes ineffective in connecting with or relating to the broader culture. Most of its resources go into the internal needs of the congregation, further cutting itself off from the brokenness of the surrounding communities. Most of the energy of the church is directed inward, losing sight of why the church exists. This self-absorption perpetuates the division between sacred and secular. This model exists in varying degrees, but each example contributes to and reinforces compartmentalization to some extent. By creating the sacred box, this style of church perpetuates the fragmentation that many Christians experience in society.

A few of my Bible Institute students mentioned how they had to renounce their love for the game of soccer to demonstrate faithfulness to Christ. One mentioned how his church leader had prohibited members from involving themselves in the men's soccer leagues, claiming them to be a "work of the devil" because they kept individuals from attending church activities. Instead, churches should not be so quick to judge but should be more open to embrace a missional perspective, looking for God's guidance in leading incarnational initiatives within their communities. The soccer leagues could provide a bridge between the church and the community.

This is not to say that there will not be challenges while taking on these initiatives. Leaders must use caution and discernment when engaging in various outreaches to make sure the congregants involved are not being influenced by the culture more than they are influencing. This could be counter-productive and could impede future outreaches. There are obvious aspects in culture that could negatively influence members, but these exceptions should not give reason to completely block the congregation from participation in the community or society at large. Missional leaders, rather, can become ambassadors in their communities, bringing reconciliation between God and the neighborhood. The church has the privilege of being God's representative in the community, serving as a mediator of his love and grace.

A Post-Church Culture

At the May 2009 Pew Forum on Religion and Public Life, top political scientists Robert Putnam and David Campbell presented research from their book *American Grace*, released last month. They reported that "young Americans are dropping out of religion at an alarming rate of five to six times the historic rate (30 to 40 percent have no religion today, versus 5 to 10 percent a generation ago)." . . . There has been a corresponding drop in church involvement. According to Rainer Research, approximately 70 percent of American youth drop out of church between 18 and 22. The Barna Group estimates that 80 percent of those reared in the church will be "disengaged" by the time they are 29.[14]

America is becoming increasingly more secular and the relevance of the church is diminishing, particularly among the disaffected younger, postmodern demographic. Even though America is becoming increasingly "churchless," the church still operates from a posture that expects outsiders to attend services on their own initiatives. This was feasible in a churched culture where most Americans attended church regularly, grew up in church, and had some understanding of the Bible. As the church in general moves from the center of society to the margins, a proactive, incarnational thrust for ministry needs to be promoted to reach an increasingly unchurched culture. Leading scholar Darrell L. Guder states, "Neither the structures nor the theology of our established Western traditional churches is missional. They are shaped by the legacy of Christendom."[15] The transition from a "Christendom" society to a "post-Christendom" society has happened, but some churches continue to operate from a passive, attractional posture despite the change. Society is moving from a mostly churched culture to a mostly unchurched culture. This shift has caused the church to lose influence in society and be pushed from the center to the margins.

---

14. Gary Tyra, *A Missional Orthodoxy: Theology and Ministry in a Post-Christian Context* (Downers Grove: IVP Academic, 2013), 37.
15. Guder, ed., *Missional Church*, 5. Craig Van Gelder prefers to use "post-church culture" instead of "post-Christendom" to distinguish between the European meaning of the term and the American popularized version. There is no question that the American church has been influenced by Christendom, but since the formal separation of church and state in the U.S. Constitution at the end of the colonial period, it is more accurate to make a distinction between the two forms. For simplicity, "post-Christendom" and "post-church culture" are used interchangeably in this book to describe the church's state of increased marginalization in the public arena.

Closing Thoughts

In an attractional model, the church is preoccupied with filling its pews to fund the costs associated with operating a centralized and established building. The priority is focused on the numerical growth of its congregation and the size of the bank account to further structural expansion. Focusing primarily on the internal needs creates a desperation to retain members, which serves to further isolate the congregation from potential spheres of influence among communities and workplaces. When the church is centripetal, or faced inwardly, it becomes ineffective in reaching the surrounding neighborhood, and, instead, requires others to yield to its agenda. Ideally, the church has the opportunity to harness an outward, centrifugal thrust, recognizing the importance of equipping and supporting its members to be missionaries in a society that no longer seeks out the church on its own initiative. This "both/and" type of church seeks to "go" make disciples but also to be the church in surrounding neighborhoods and workplaces. This type of church is set on gathering (centripetal) to be encouraged, equipped, and empowered so they can be missionaries the rest of the week (centrifugal) in areas where the members are in the minority. A pro-active, outward approach like this will cause the church to be more effective in reaching an increasingly unchurched society in today's post-Christendom culture.

Biblical Insights

When Israel finally transitioned into the Promised Land, they attained a sense of permanency and notoriety. The transition from the Tabernacle to the Temple was symbolic of Israel's transition from being a nomadic people to an established monarchy. Under the leadership of Solomon, Israel equated God's call, as Bryan Stone explains, with "military might, geographical expansion, economic affluence, and an imperial mindset."[16] He also adds, "What it means to be the people of God can never be something static, finished, fortresslike, or permanent. Indeed, exile and diaspora may

---

16. Bryan P. Stone, *Evangelism after Christendom: The Theology and Practice of Christian Witness* (Grand Rapids: Brazos Press, 2007), 1202, Kindle.

very well be the 'normal' existence, even the vocation, of the people of God."[17] Thus, the call and election of Yahweh were never intended to be only for the benefit of Israel to the exclusion of other nations. The prophets in the Old Testament reminded Israel about their special election and chosen status, but also exhorted them not to forget but to remember their missionary purpose. God's love for Israel has always been inclusive of other nations. As Stone explains, "There can be no trade-off between God's calling of and love for Israel, on the one hand, and God's purpose and love for the world, on the other."[18] Gregory Beale pens the following regarding an inclusive call for all of God's people to join him in his ongoing mission to all nations:

> Exodus 19:6 says that Israel collectively was to be to God "a kingdom of priests and a holy nation," going out to the nations and being mediators between God and the nations by bearing God's light of revelation. Instead of seeing the temple as a symbol of their task to expand God's presence to all nations, Israel wrongly viewed the temple to be symbolic of their election as God's only true people and that God's presence was to be restricted only to them as an ethnic nation.[19]

When God's people established an earthly kingdom in the Old Testament, their comfort and prominence were disrupted. In Gen. 11:9, the Lord "confused the language of the whole earth; and from there the LORD scattered them abroad over the face of the whole earth." The building project became a distraction from God's mission for the nations when the builders became focused on their own interests and plans. Stone attests, "The intention of the builders was to gather the people into a centralized

---

17. Stone, *Evangelism after Christendom*, 2210, Kindle. Stone quotes from John Howard Yoder's book, *For the Nations: Essays Public and Evangelical* (Grand Rapids, Eerdmans, 1997), 55-60.
18. Stone, *Evangelism after Christendom*, 1237, Kindle.
19. Gregory K. Beale, "Eden, the Temple, and the Church's Mission in the New Creation," *JETS* 48/1 (March 2005): 15, accessed April 2, 2015, *ATLA Religion Database with ATLASerials*, EBSCO*host*.

location, thereby resisting God's purpose that they should multiply, fill the earth, and subdue it."[20] In Christopher Wright's words, the Babel account is a depiction of the fallen human heart "intent on reaching the heavens even while resisting God's will for them on earth."[21] Yahweh interfered with this building project and acted by scattering the builders over the whole earth, not only to multiply, fill, and subdue it, but to be a blessing to the nations. God's people were tasked to be a light to the nations, giving glory to Yahweh only, and inviting others into a loving relationship with their creator.

Words and Phrases to Remember

Attractional: This church seeks to draw "outsiders" to attend one of its scheduled services by attracting them. The church is heavily focused inwardly, causing it to become blind to the greater mission of God in its communities and workplaces. This model worked in a society with a built-in disposition to seek out the church, but it has become an ineffective posture in an increasingly unchurched society.

Key Verses to Reflect

Gen. 11:9
Ex. 19:6
Phil. 2:3-5

Discovery Questions

1. How are some ways that you can better connect to others outside of your church without an agenda?

---

20. Christopher J. H. Wright, *The Mission of God: Unlocking the Bible's Grand Narrative* (Downers Grove: InterVarsity, 2006), 201.
21. Wright, *The Mission of God*, 197.

The Attractional Model

2. Describe how too much attention to "building, butts, and budget" can negatively affect the church's outreach.

3. What is a "member culture" and how do attractional churches foster this?

4. How can attractional churches negatively encourage compartmentalization in the lives of their members?

CHAPTER 2

The Missional Model

SHARING LIFE TOGETHER

WHEN JOHN'S WIFE ASKED HIM about his good friend Leonard, he responded, "I just want my friend back." Leonard had failed to realize that the biggest impact he could have on John was to continue to be his friend; then, through the bond that they shared, Leonard would be able to introduce Christ to John. Through normal interaction and communication, Leonard would be John's initial experience of church. With a missional mindset, evangelism is not reduced to getting outsiders to come to church and sign on as members. Instead, through the friendship and trust, people like Leonard learn to journey with friends like John as they share their lives together. The conversation about faith and church attendance should arise naturally and informally.

The best sermon that John could ever hear is the testimony of Leonard's transformed life when Leonard lets his light shine instead of hiding his new life in Christ under the "church umbrella." Unfortunately, the attractional model has the potential of influencing its members in such a way that they become overly absorbed with the church's internal life, which causes members to lose sight of their broader mission back to their communities. Members will have limited impact on their acquaintances, family, and friends if they do not have the margin to connect with them in meaningful ways. The places where church members live and work are where they spend the bulk of their lives and have the most significant influence. In Leonard's case, he had lost sight of the incredible opportunity he had to invest into the life of a friend he had known for many years. Instead, he could have learned to interact with his old friend, John, with a new perspective on life. He could have learned to align his life with Kingdom principles and encourage his best friend to do likewise.

The role of Leonard's church family is to support and encourage him to live a missional life in his own community. In this context, Leonard could learn to be part of a network of "missionaries," dispersed to the hardest-to-reach places in the city, starting in his own neighborhood. Instead of functioning within a building, the church would function as a decentralized, relational web where God's Spirit works in creative and unifying ways. Instead of the church remaining centralized and static, it could be set free to approach ministry in different ways. With an outward thrust, the body of Christ becomes intentional about connecting with outsiders like John. The glue that holds the church together, then, is the network of maturing relationships and the presence of God's Spirit working through the body of Christ.

AN OUTWARD THRUST

Counter to the attractional model is the missional model where the energy is directed outward rather than inward. This posture is "centrifugal" rather than "centripetal" because it takes seriously the Great Commission of going and making disciples of all nations, starting in their own community and extending out from there. The missional church realizes that the unchurched may never walk through their doors, so for this reason, it is necessary for them to represent Christ away from the officially sanctioned building. When they gather, it is not to retain individuals and box them in, but, rather, the gathered church is set on equipping and supporting its people to be local missionaries to their communities. The posture of this outward thrust creates a tension with the attractional church because it does not guarantee growth in the number of members. The missional church releases its members, realizing that they are the ones who can be most effective in reaching their communities—where they live and work—beyond the church walls.

Beach describes one congregant's confession after his experience with an outward-oriented church: "It was the support of his church community in midst of his doubt that made it possible for him to once again confess Christ as Lord and determine to engage in the mission of Christ with a newfound enthusiasm."[22] Members need the church to provide the revitalization to live faithfully in the arenas where they spend most of their time and have the greatest influence. Typically, members spend the bulk of their life away from the church grounds, so this arena becomes their mission field. In the attractional church, the focus on the internal programming can have a blinding effect to the mission beyond those walls.

A Missional Mindset

For many of the students I taught at various Bible institutes, ministry had been reduced to their involvement and participation in the various programs and activities on church grounds. I thought that these students were the perfect candidates for this transition toward becoming missional leaders because they were passionate to serve the Lord with their whole heart; but I also felt they were not serving at their full potential. Even though most of their lives were spent in their neighborhoods and workplaces, many developed a mental model of ministry that kept them from seeing these contexts as having enormous potential to put their gifts and talents to work. This mindset was troubling considering these were the places in which they had greatest influence and, thus, could be viewed as their mission fields. They were lacking a missional mindset that allowed them to see the places outside of the church building as places for ministry and "ripe fields ready to be harvested" (Jn. 4:35). It became evident that missional training was a void that, if implemented, could transform their understanding of ministry. Having a missional mindset meant that they would begin to see themselves as local missionaries sent out to their communities and workplaces to share their lives and the gospel beyond the church building.

Sent Out as Missionaries

In moving toward becoming missional, the church has the opportunity to reprioritize to avoid being focusing entirely on the internal life of the

---

22. Beach, *The Church in Exile*, 3291, Kindle.

Christian community. As Beach states, the church should "also include an outward thrust that takes seriously the missional nature of God's people and Christ's call for his church to be a people who go into the world."[23] In this model, the church is not trying to retain individuals and cause them to stay; instead, it seeks to equip and empower its people with the training and encouragement they need so they can "go," making disciples in their neighborhoods and workplaces. When the church gathers, it is not to isolate the body from the world; rather, it is to be armed and sent out as missionaries the rest of the week in the spheres where the church is the minority. In this way, the church is balanced between centripetal and centrifugal postures of ministry. The church gathers for fellowship and edification, but it also realizes that ministry will take place primarily as members go about their lives engaging the world. The gathering of the church should lead to a scattering among neighborhoods and workplaces to be salt and light in the world (Mt. 5:13-16).

Measure of Success

Generally speaking, the church isn't interested in isolating its members from their communities so that they will not be able to impact their families, friends, and neighbors with the gospel message. However, perhaps it is time to change the mindset that the church is a place to which individuals go; rather, the church is comprised of God's people, who can be equipped and sent out to impact their communities for the sake of the Kingdom. When the church is attractional, the focus is on assimilating congregants into various programs and activities. This culture is heavily reliant on drawing people into the church, the inward focus of which is essential for it to reach its numerical goals. The ability to draw people into the officially sanctioned church is the primary measure of success for the attractional model.

Because success is often measured on their ability to draw people in and fill the pews during scheduled services, it is difficult for pastors to be

---

23. Beach, *The Church in Exile*, 2903, Kindle.

more outwardly focused. Being outwardly focused goes against the established measures of success for the attractional church, so leaders will naturally spend their energy to draw people inside. When church leaders speak to one another, one of the first topics that come up in conversation is the size of their congregations. Pastors with the largest churches receive notoriety and recognition. They receive awards at their denominational conferences for their financial contributions toward programs operated from the central offices. These leaders are typically the ones who are invited to speak at conferences and events about their numerical accomplishments, creating a culture that measures success on the three "Bs": butts in the seats, bank accounts, and building size. Their centripetal force of "drawing" worshippers creates a self-preserving dialectical tension with the missional mode's centrifugal force of "sending" missionaries to reach their own communities through their lives and the gospel. The missional model follows the pattern of the Godhead—the Father sent his Son, the Son sent the Holy Spirit, who now empowers and sends out the church on mission locally and globally. Below is a table comparing the attractional and missional models:

Table 1. Attractional Versus Missional Model

Attractional	Missional
Inward-Focused	Outward-Focused
Centralized presence of God	The church is the temple of the Holy Spirit
Retention	Mission
Established and permanent	Mobile and loose
Buildings, budget, and butts	Minimal overhead
Religious life revolves around location	Little reliance on location
Church is something people go to	People take the church wherever they go

THE MISSIONAL CHURCH

Missional scholars Frost and Hirsch define missional as follows:

> A missional church is one whose primary commitment is to the missionary calling of the people of God. As such, it is one that aligns itself with God's missionary purposes in the world. A missional leader is one that takes mission seriously and sees it as the driving energy behind all the church does. The missional church is a sent church with one of its defining values being the development of a church life and practice that is contextualized to that culture to which it believes it is sent.[24]

The missional model sees God as the missionary who sends the church into the world. Mission is not only a program or department of the local church but the foundation for why the church exists. The missional model sees the Bible, from Genesis to Revelation, as God acting in the world, seeking to save fallen creation. South African missionary David Bosch went so far as to write, "Mission is the mother of all theology."[25] God is a missionary God, so the church is comprised of a missionary people. With this is mind, leaders can find comfort in the realization that their Christian duty is not to manufacture a mission but only to participate in what their missionary God is doing in their midst.

Instead of the church being at the center of mission, everything that the body is involved in revolves around the mission of God. The church is not the one initiating or fabricating mission; rather, it only participates in what God is already doing. Consequently, instead of hoping that God will bless their efforts, it is important for those seeking to follow Christ to have their hearts and minds attuned to what he is already doing in their midst. Any efforts on the church's behalf of bringing reconciliation and redemption to others starts with him. His authority and power are essential to any outreach.

---

24. Frost and Hirsch, *The Shaping of Things to Come*, 229.
25. David J. Bosch, *Transforming Mission: Paradigm Shifts in Theology of Mission* (Maryknoll, NY: Orbis Books, 2009), 16.

The Father sent his Son to fulfill the mission of redeeming, restoring, and reconciling creation. The Father and Son sent the Holy Spirit to empower the church to go into the world to fulfill God's mission. Jesus's mission to redeem humanity continues through the creation of a community of disciples that help grow the church. The Holy Spirit is the guide who "will teach you all things and will remind you of everything I have said to you" (John 14:26, NIV).[26] The Holy Spirit teaches the church the ways of the Son. The church is now the temple of the Holy Spirit, meaning the Christian community is where God's presence resides. Church is not a place, but it is the living presence of God through his believing community. The Holy Spirit resides inside the hearts and minds of the believing community. The church participates and joins God in his ongoing mission. This should be good news to the church!

Any study of ecclesiology (church theology) without the study of missiology (the mission of God) is a contradiction. As missiologist David Bosch writes about the church, "Its mission is not secondary to its being."[27] There are certainly some attractional components of Jesus's ministry as he drew people to himself for healing, redemption, and reconciliation (Mt. 7:25; 15:21-28; Mk. 7:25, Lk. 8:43). These Kingdom-building moments, however, were manifested on the move, reaching out and engaging people in their homes, neighborhoods, and marketplaces. Jesus's objective was not to build a brick and mortar kingdom where people could come and find him. Instead, he took the gospel with him on his journeys and encountered individuals where they were. According to Frost and Hirsch, the "come-to-us" mentality possessed by attractional churches "is unbiblical. It's not found in the Gospels or the Epistles."[28] An attractional model can be detrimental to the mission of God when the church becomes inward-focused. Religious life revolves around meeting its own needs instead of joining God in his plans and purposes.

---

26. Unless otherwise noted, all scriptures will be from the New King James Version (NKJV).
27. Bosch. *Transforming Mission*, 372.
28. Frost and Hirsch, *The Shaping of Things to Come*, 19.

Building Bridges

In a missional model, the objective of coming together is not to focus on itself and further isolate the church from the world. Instead, the inner life of the church seeks to be centrifugal and spread out and be dispersed outward. Eddie Gibbs and Ryan Bolger propose the need for the church to "create bridges that span the secular/sacred divide" and to see "the sacredness of all of life."[29] The intent is to take the gospel of Christ and share the message of hope in unreached places, typically in the spheres of life where Christians are already living and some level of influence is already established. It is when the daily life of the church becomes infused within society that the gospel can best be demonstrated and proclaimed. This is not a quick-fix solution to ministry but requires intentionality to embody the life of Christ in all realms of life. When the church bridges the sacred and secular compartments of life, it lives with greater integrity in all arenas within and outside of church grounds.

It is difficult for churchgoers to embody the love of Christ if they are not seeking to represent him in their communities and workplaces. How will the unchurched hear the good news if the church is absorbed in its own internal life with all its activities and programming? Members need to be empowered and released so they can journey with others outside of the church's fold. They are the ones who will be reaching and teaching their friends, family, and acquaintances to follow Christ, realizing his salvific plan for their lives. In this sense, evangelism moves away from practices associated with attempting to attract outsiders to a building, program, or event. Instead, Christian leaders pursue whole-life evangelism where every facet of their lives would be transformed and brought into service as a witness for the glory of God. Outsiders would notice the difference in the lives of believers, not primarily because they go to church, but because of a genuine transformation as they exhibit the fruits of the Spirit and Christlikeness in all areas of life. Church attendance is not the mark of a mature Christian

---

29. Eddie Gibbs and Ryan K. Bolger, *Emerging Churches: Creating Christian Community in Postmodern Cultures* (Grand Rapids: Baker Academic, 2005), 67-68.

but a transformed mind and heart manifested by following Christ into this broken world.

Incarnational Ministry

Gibbs and Bolger write, "We are commanded by Christ as his followers to live incarnationally, to overcome boundaries, to express the God-life, and to recognize where God is at work in every realm."[30] Church members are often consumed with the demands of life. Work, school, family, recreation, civic duties, and other facets of life can stretch any family's schedule. Often, all the various programs and activities of the church leave little margin for members to have an impact in their own contexts, in the places where they spend most of their time. An attractional church pulls its people into the building and the church agenda to the extent that they become ineffective in their own communities. The only associations believers will have if they are constantly being pulled into the religious bubble are with people who think, act, and speak the same way. A missional-minded church sees the role of its members as missionaries to the arenas of life where they have frequent contact with the unchurched.

A way forward is to form believing communities in the places where members spend the most time, which are the home, workplace, or neighborhood. Recently, I heard a colleague say, "You cannot commute to your mission field." Individuals live in one neighborhood, work in another, play in another, and sometimes commute clear across town to do "church" in another section of town. Americans live such compartmentalized lives that it is hard to be fully present in any of these places. With this mentality, as well intentioned as some may be, it will be difficult to make a lasting impact either in the community that is near one's church or in one's own neighborhood. The real mission in attractional churches remains directed to the churchgoers who come from all parts of town to be ministered to by the professional ministers. Member engagement in spiritual matters is usually for a few hours a week, after which they commute back home when

---

30. Gibbs and Bolger, *Emerging Churches*, 75.

services are over. They do not make any impact in the community where their church is located nor in their own neighborhood because they are pulled away from it by the frequent gatherings.

Ideally, clusters of believers would form naturally beyond the church walls as the church scatters and commits to sharing the good news with those around them through word and deed. This stands in contrast to attempting to extract and isolate members from their communities and workplaces. This effect would be diminished if there were more missionaries sent out from local congregations intentional about forming communities of faith on the turf of the unchurched which are the places where they work and live. This approach requires members to seek relationships and share their faith as a normal part of their life in the places where they spend the most time. This leads to whole-life evangelism, where all of one's life becomes a testimony and gives glory to God, instead of an occasional event based on the church's weekly calendar.

This will require members willing to engage their communities with boldness as they see the mission field that is right before their eyes. This requires a good testimony among their coworkers and neighbors, which goes beyond a few hours a week during one of the church services. It is easy to be on one's best behavior for a few hours a week when the church gathers for fellowship. It requires greater commitment to Christ when believers are called to be salt and light in the trenches of life. Being Christlike in the grind of a work week requires a strong commitment to the Lord when heavy traffic, difficult neighbors, and unreasonable bosses are thrown into the mix. To influence others in a positive manner and not become disqualified, members are required to exhibit the fruits of the Spirit as representatives of Christ in the world. The church cannot be two-faced, one way on Sunday morning and another way on Monday morning. Following Jesus's commission will not be easy and he cautions his disciples that they are being sent out as lambs among wolves in a broken and unmerciful world. Yet even during trials and tribulations, Jesus tells his disciples, "Be of good cheer, for I have overcome the world."

AN EXAMPLE TO FOLLOW

A man I deeply respect attempted to live his Christian walk in all realms of his life by moving into an impoverished neighborhood in one of Houston's predominantly black sectors. I read a few of his books, and he is regarded within Christian academia as one of the top-tier writers in America addressing the problem of racism in the evangelical church. His work is groundbreaking and shows the acute disparities between white and black neighborhoods in the country. He brings light to the racial tensions within the evangelical church in America by having interviewed hundreds of participants in his study. Obviously, his dedication toward his calling has caused me to have great admiration toward him. I had the privilege of hearing his insights about the racial inequalities in the Houston area during a lecture he conducted at my seminary.

Even though he had acquired many accolades and had received national recognition for his work, he moved into one of the worst parts of town with his family. Even though he had good reason and the means to live in a white suburb, he and his family were the only white people in a predominantly black neighborhood known for its poverty and crime. This was the message that had the most profound impact on me, much more than the other scholarly achievements for which he had been recognized. This is what being incarnational is all about, following the example of Jesus who "made Himself of no reputation, taking the form of a servant, even though he was equal with God" (Phil. 2:6-7).[31] This man left the comfort and security of the affluent suburbs to be obedient to the calling of God in his life. He dwelt among the people group he had dedicated much of his life to defend.

SURRENDERING CONTROL

When individuals take steps to be incarnational, they become vulnerable and at the mercy of those whom they are seeking to reach since they are entering their home turf. In the attractional church, the impetus is

---

31. Unless otherwise noted, all scriptures will be from the New King James Version (NKJV).

attempting to invite the unchurched to leave their communities and find fellowship with Christians. This means that the church keeps the power and control when outsiders are the ones asked to be vulnerable and approach the churched on their terms and turf. As long as the unchurched yield to the church's agenda, the church is hospitable to them when they come through the front doors. It does not require supernatural love to make outsiders feel welcomed and embraced when they leave their turf to meet the church in their territory. This is a "come to us" approach to ministry, where the church holds a passive posture requiring the unchurched to take the first step, instead of the church taking the initiative to meet them where they are on their turf. It takes a certain level of vulnerability and surrender to be placed at the mercy of those one seeks to reach. Even when Christ was equal with God, he made himself of no reputation, took the form of a bondservant, humbled himself, and dwelt among sinners (Phil. 2:6-7). Jesus did not expect for humanity to rise up to meet him. He did not ask the world he came to save to meet him in the middle, but he came down all the way as a mortal, relinquishing his rights as God. The same posture exemplified by Christ is to be continued by the church. Missional leaders go into the world and become outsiders, hoping that eventually they can win the people's trust, eventually resulting in a relationship with Christ. It requires surrender because the results are left in the hands of Christ. These leaders dwell among the groups they hope to reach with the gospel even when they face rejection and opposition with the hope of making Christ's name known.

ON THEIR TURF

An inward focus places the interest of the church first. Attractional churches require the unchurched to embody the culture of Christians. In contrast, an incarnational posture is "always inclined to go forth and enter into the lives of a host community,"[32] on their terms, not the church's. This is not only a pattern set by Christ but is also a suitable approach in a society that is not seeking out the church. In a society where churchgo-

---

32. Gibbs and Bolger, *Emerging Churches*, 75.

ing is not a normal part of life, relinquishing one's interests and goals, and putting others' needs first is a posture of humility reflected through the life of Jesus. Some fear taking their faith to the public realm because they risk facing rejection and opposition. It was for this reason that Jesus made it clear to his disciples, "In the world you will have tribulation" (Jn. 16:33), and "You will be hated by all for my name's sake" (Mt. 10:22). He also reassured them that they would never be alone (Mt. 28:20) and that he would never abandon them (Heb. 13:5). He never attempted to paint a rosy picture but was honest with his disciples about the hostility they would face because of their devotion to him. Jesus himself faced opposition in the world while fulfilling his calling. Likewise, Christians should expect to encounter resistance as they enter unchartered territory with the intent of spreading the message of good news, but they also can expect God's presence to be with them.

No longer can the church expect the unchurched to conform to its agenda. Hoping to grow in number of attendees, the attractional church seeks to draw and lure outsiders. Expecting them to approach the sanctuary, however, requires the unchurched to be incarnational toward believers. A missional approach passionately engages the community without expecting anything in return. It requires relinquishing one's desires and ambitions to win some to Christ on their terms. Being incarnational does not guarantee numerical growth, but it also does not mean the church body will not grow. The attractional model uses numerical growth of the church as its primary measure of success. It looks at the quantity of seats being filled during the scheduled service hours. In contrast, the missional church measures success by the relationships and lives being transformed by the gospel in the communities they seek to serve.

Social Media
Social media is an avenue where the church can connect with people from their communities and across the globe. This relatively new social tool offers the church a means to connect with the unchurched in ways they would not be able to accomplish otherwise. An acquaintance

of mine expressed his concerns about being on Facebook because, in his words, "There were too many 'worldly' people on this social media outlet." He spent most of his time making sure the only friends he had on his account were other believers because he did not want to be tainted or influenced by evildoers. Of course, there are some real dangers on social media and believers should be wary. A well-grounded believer, however, need not take such an antagonistic view toward the general population. This man had been walking with the Lord for some time and would do well to seek opportunities to make an impact in the lives of others who are far from God. If we use social media outlets only to engage people who behave and act like us, then we exist in our own spiritual bubbles and become ineffective in influencing others in a positive way. With technology, the church can reach the ends of the earth as it never could before, making disciples of all nations by starting among those in their own communities.

As stated, it is wise to have safeguards when on social media and be cognizant of the dangers lurking on the web "taking heed lest we fall." Additionally, believers should take precaution and create their own accountability measures so they can be called out by trusted friends if needed. However, technology can provide a way to be incarnational, connecting with others who otherwise would be unreachable or who would never set foot in a church building. Being in the world but not of the world is a tension that believers seek to maintain as they pursue faithfulness to the Great Commission. It would be counterproductive to seek to influence the world and, in the process, fall victim to the temptations it offers, especially on social media. In one case, a pastor attempted to reach out to others on social media, but fell into an adulterous relationship from the pull of an attractive woman. This relationship cost him everything—his family, respect within his community, and his position as pastor.

TRANSITIONING TOWARD MISSIONAL

This section will provide some practical examples for leaders as they begin taking strides toward a more outward-focused, missional posture in their churches. For several years, I worked in declining, attractional churches in various contexts. I wholeheartedly believed that survival hinged on their ability to move toward missional thinking. Transitioning toward a missional posture comes with struggles and barriers, the strongest of which are the embedded attractional modes of operation that have been in existence for decades making change difficult. In some contexts, it is easier to start from scratch than to try to move an attractional church toward missional. Especially in some of the older congregations where there is substantial history and heritage within the church. Changing the DNA of a church could take years, and the pastor will most likely encounter continued resistance on behalf of the members who may have only an attractional mental mindset.

The following are a few practical steps that can be implemented progressively, so as not to overwhelm the congregation with changes that seem drastic. A pastor could gradually make these modifications in transitioning an inward-focused church toward becoming missional:

1. **The church looks like the community:** The missional church creates an inclusive environment where people feel safe and accepted. The church would take seriously the demographic changes that have taken place in recent years and relinquish power to allow something new to blossom. In some contexts, even though the neighborhood's demographic make-up has completely transformed, the church is not intentional about reaching the people represented in their midst. Church leaders would take steps to increase their own and the congregation's cultural intelligence and community awareness. Oftentimes, members commute long distances from the suburbs from neighborhoods within the same socio-economic and racial background. This makes it difficult to assimilate and be incarnational in the church's own backyard. The church would do well to shape itself according to the context it is called to reach instead of expecting outsiders to change and conform to the way they think, act, and speak.

2. **The church would have community-focused ministries:** A missional church would initiate or partner with community-based outreaches that seek to bring wholeness to the brokenness in the neighborhood. The church would be intentional about meeting a real need in the community and focus less on meeting their own needs. Through their service, opportunities to share the gospel message would arise. It would reevaluate its own ministries that seek to meet only an inward need to make available resources for other evangelistic initiatives. The church would stop focusing so much on being attractive as a growth strategy and find ways to serve the community through connecting with outsiders. The church would make attempts to be involved in the school system, local businesses, civic organizations, and other groups where they can connect with the community. Instead of reinventing the wheel, the church would partner with some already established non-profits in the area. Instead of attempting to get others to join their programs, the church would collaborate with others outside of their circle.
3. **The church building is not the center of religious life.** The church building would be a missional outpost where emphasis is given to training, planning, and strategizing for impact in the community and workplace. "Church is not a Sunday morning event, but a place where God's people learn to be committed to God's mission in their community. The building is a gathering place where members are encouraged and equipped so they can be missionaries the rest of the week. Consecrating a building as the only legitimate expression of God's presence would not be encouraged. The church would encourage and support outward initiatives, which would allow them to engage others outside of their typical gathering.
4. **There would be a pendulum swing in finances toward external objectives.** The clergy would initiate fundraising events that address issues in the community. They would assess their church's

budget, even if it includes evaluating their own salaries in order to meet missional objectives. The possibility of the clergy becoming bi-vocational should be considered, especially when the church is struggling financially. Plans to allot an increased amount of the church's budget toward community initiatives will be hindered unless the expenditures on internal programs, activities, and clergy salaries are reevaluated. Clergy would seek additional means of income, becoming less reliant on the church's budget, and members could then take on greater responsibilities in the church. Ultimately, having bi-vocational clergy would reduce some of the pressure on the congregants to fulfill the church's financial needs. A long-term goal would be to get closer to 50% of the church's budget directed toward internal programming and clergy salaries and the rest allocated toward outward projects and initiatives. The pastors would be criticized less because they would not depend so heavily on the church's finances, freeing some of the burden. It would also give the pastors more freedom in their input on the direction for the church, since they would be less influenced by the people paying their salaries. Board members would spend less time discussing the inward concerns of the church and more time on missional objectives.

5. **The church would take prayer seriously.** Prayer would become central to the life of the church. Taking prayer seriously would help the church discern how the Holy Spirit is leading them to serve in their communities. Prayer meetings would happen inside the church but also outside the walls of the building. Praying for someone in the hospital would mean physically being in his or her room. The offering of prayer would not be limited to the church's members, their friends and families, and their physical needs. Missional prayers would incorporate asking God how the church could be utilized to bring wholeness to the needs of others, especially the unchurched in their vicinity. The church would be intentional about discerning how they are

to actively participate with God in addressing the brokenness in their community.

6. **The pastor is not the only minister of the church.** The members of the church would begin to see themselves in the category of the "priesthood of believers" (1 Pet. 2:5-9). The ministry functions would not be reserved only for the pastor, but members would carry out a more active role. The members would become more involved in the priestly roles of praying, visiting the sick, leading Bible studies, and others. Ministry would be shared among the members and each person would begin to discover and apply his or her gifts and talents. The pastor would serve to empower others by reaffirming the gifts of the laymen and their roles in outreach. Members would no longer be passive but would be intentional about serving in their spheres of influence, including their workplaces, homes, and communities.

7. **The church is clear about its purpose.** The church's vision and mission would be clearer and it would begin to nurture a missional DNA. With increased clarity, the church would feel excited and passionate about its reason for existence. The mission would fulfill a real need and would bring healing, restoration, and reconciliation to brokenness within the community. The creative juices of the church would begin to flow, and the church would be energized due to its compelling vision. The members would feel that they are a part of that vision instead of just trying to help the pastor achieve his own vision. When the church focuses outside instead of inside, arguments could potentially decrease because members would feel a sense of united purpose. Members would be too busy carrying out compelling missional objectives and they would not want to waste time bickering with one another.

8. **The members are not stuck in the glory days.** Because of their rich heritage, some attractional churches fight to maintain their traditions–the way things have always been. The "old timers" would loosen their grip on maintaining the practices of the

past, including singing from hymnals, for example, and be open to new and innovative ways of being a church. Not only would these long-time members give up some of their control, but they would also encourage and nourish new disciples who so desperately are striving to fit in. The pastor would create ways in which congregants can feel connected to the past but simultaneously find ways to allow the new to blossom. The building and all of its relics have been part of the contention characterizing attractional churches. Oftentimes, there can be intense emotions when people feel like their heritage is in jeopardy.

9. **Quality and not quantity.** Success would not be measured by the numbers but by the church's ability to stay true to what they have been called to do. Their actions would align with their mission statement, regardless of the number of people drawn into the services on Sunday morning. Their mission would not be something that is manufactured; rather, they would participate with God and his mission in the community where the church exists to be a light and to give glory to God. The church's main mission would shift toward a discernment process to discover where God was already at work rather than fabricating a mission that God might bless. Developing relationships within the community would be prioritized over measuring attendance.

10. **Transformational leadership.** The church leadership would move from program managers to missional leaders. They would be intentional about growing in missional capacity in order to train others as well. The church leadership would be the first on the journey of transition, thus increasing their ability to obtain buy-in from the members. The church leadership would loosen their grip on their members. They would be intentional about equipping and empowering themselves and others so that they could send their congregation out as local missionaries to their communities. Those, who have already led a church through a transition, can be solicited in helping the church navigate new, missional waters.

11. **Missional theology.** Mission would be viewed as the "mother of all theology," in the words of missiologist Bosch.[33] From Genesis to Revelation, the theme of God seeking to redeem his broken creation would be emphasized through preaching and teaching. The congregation would learn to see through a missional lens, which could impact chamber meetings, soccer fields, high school football games, and more in order to break the divide between the secular and sacred compartments of life. They would learn their roles in God's redemptive plan in their community.

CLOSING THOUGHTS

Leading scholar Darrell L. Guder states, "Neither the structures nor the theology of our established Western traditional churches is missional. They are shaped by the legacy of Christendom."[34] The culture, of which he speaks, fosters a conception of ministry as exclusively inside the sanctioned building. "Service to the Lord" is confined to volunteering in one of the programs or activities of the local church. When the people of God become focused on themselves and church-centered, what follows is a pulling away from the world. In contrast, with a missional mindset, the church becomes a sent people called to engage culture and share their lives and the gospel.

Additionally, full-time ministry positions are often reserved for the ordained, professional ministers who serve primarily inside the formal church building in an attractional posture. In a churched culture, this posture was acceptable when most Americans attended church regularly, grew up in church, and had some understanding of the Bible. As the church in general moves from the center of society to the margins, the laity must be trained in a way that will promote a proactive, incarnational, missional thrust. No longer is it feasible to foster a culture where service to the Lord, however sincere and dedicated, is confined to involvement in

---

33. Bosch, *Transforming Mission*, 16.
34. Darrel L. Guder, ed., *Missional Church: A Vision for the Sending of the Church in North America* (Grand Rapids: Eerdmans, 1998), 5.

the programs and activities of the local church. The laity, in turn, will experience a broadening of their horizons in terms of new opportunities for Kingdom ministry. Church leaders play an integral role in guiding others on their journey to "explore their significance for the manifold ministries of the people of God in the world."[35]

In a missional mode, the energy is directed outward. The church is not trying to cause individuals to stay, assimilate, and get comfortable; instead, the church seeks to "go" and make disciples, to be incarnational in their neighborhoods and workplaces. When the church gathers, it is not to retain individuals and attempt to get them to align with the church's objectives and agenda. Rather, the church gathers to equip and support its members to be missionaries in their neighborhoods and workplaces. The thrust is not directed inward; rather, the church gathers to disperse energy outward. This means that leaders relinquish control of their people, seeking, instead, to "build up the body" in order to send them into the world as missionaries. Church leaders recognize the vastness of talents and giftings represented in the church body. They seek to encourage and develop others to discover and fulfill their God-given roles in the world.

BIBLICAL INSIGHTS

It is futile to attempt to be missional without looking at Jesus. There are many examples of well-intended missional pioneers who become so wrapped up in the movement that they miss the heart of the matter. The focus becomes on being relevant and innovative to the point that the responsibility to the gospel is compromised. The lure of the missional movement entices believers to the appeal of something cutting edge, but if Jesus is not at the center, any missional movement is empty. Jesus is "the reference point for all genuine knowing, all true loving, and all authentic following of God."[36] If people want to know God, they must look to Jesus—the image of God. From this understanding, all expressions of

---
35. Eddie Gibbs, *Church Morph: How Megatrends are Reshaping Christian Communities* (Grand Rapids: Baker Academics, 2009), 52.
36. Frost and Hirsch, *The Shaping of Things to Come*, 37.

missional enterprise take form. The incarnation of Christ is a profound theological concept that comprises the core of the missional enterprise.

The best example, and the one Christians should seek to emulate in being incarnational, is the Son of God himself. Jesus "made Himself of no reputation, taking the form of a bondservant, and coming in the likeness of men" (Phil. 2:7, NKJV). Even though he was fully God, he humbled himself and became fully human. In this act, "God entered into our world and into the human condition in the person of Jesus Christ."[37] In Jn. 1:14, the author writes, "The word became flesh and made his dwelling [Greek, *skēnoō*] among us." In other words, Jesus "tabernacled" or "pitched a tent" among humanity.[38] He left his throne, where he was seated at the right hand of the Father, and made his residence among the people he came to save.

He was accessible to people in the various communities he visited (Mt. 8:28-34, 15:21-28; Lk. 7:1-10), and he had compassion on them. He emptied himself and became a mere human, a bondservant (Phil. 2:7); he assimilated himself within the culture. He was immersed in the culture and became a mere mortal. He was a devout Jew, carpenter, spoke the language, and even had a family. His objective was not to build a brick and mortar Kingdom; his Kingdom was not intended to be a physical structure where his presence could be found. Instead, Jesus took the gospel with him on his journeys and encountered individuals where they were. He preached the gospel and healed many as he travelled with his disciples from place to place. In the same way that Christ went forth, leaving his residence in heaven, churches are to leave their turf and become vulnerable in their own communities, not expecting the unchurched to submit to their plans. The church cannot be passive and expect others to come to them but must follow the example of Jesus.

The word "incarnation" originates from the act of God entering the created but fallen world in the form of a mere human living among

---

37. Ibid., 35.
38. R. E. Averbeck, "Tabernacle," in *Dictionary of the Old Testament Pentateuch*, 825.

sinners. Incarnational ministries seek to follow the example of Christ. He "made himself nothing, taking the very nature of a servant" and "being found in appearance as a man, he humbled himself and became obedient to death" (Phil. 2:7-8, NIV). Following this pattern of self-denial, Christian leaders leave their turf and comfort zones, "embodying the culture and life of a host culture in order to reach that group of people with Jesus's love."[39] The church that seeks to be incarnational does not live out of selfish ambition, placing their own desires first. The church's relationship with the world is not contingent on outsiders going to their turf.

Words and Phrases to Remember

Missional: A church model where the energy is directed outward. The church is not trying to box itself in; instead, the church seeks to "go" and make disciples, and to be the church for the people who may never walk through the doors of an officially sanctioned building.

Centrifugal: When the momentum of the church's inner life is thrust outward.

Incarnational: A posture that is always inclined to go forth and enter the lives of a host community. This posture reflects the pattern of Christ who left his heavenly domain and lived among sinful humanity as a mortal.

Key Verses to Reflect

Mt. 28:19
Phil. 2:7-8
Jn. 1:14

---

39. Frost and Hirsch, *The Shaping of Things to Come*, 228.

DISCOVERY QUESTIONS

1. What are some practices in your church that you consider to be missional?

2. How are some ways you can be more incarnational in your life?

3. Who are some people you know who have relinquished some of their privileges in order to connect and show solidarity with the people in underdeveloped communities?

TRANSITION TWO
From Rigid to Flexible Space

———◆———

THE SECOND TRANSITION INVOLVES A different way of thinking about the use of sacred space. The church seems to be stuck in rigid patterns in terms of the usage of sacred space, which has kept it from thinking about more flexible, creative solutions.

CHAPTER 3

The Central Worship Site

BUILD IT AND THEY WILL COME

VISIBLE FROM THE FREEWAY, a large church sign reads, "God is in the house, you can be too." Clearly, this promotes the idea that when drivers see the sign, it will prompt them to stop and go through the front doors to meet God. The reasoning behind placing a highly visible sign is, "We need drivers to see the sign and once they know where we are they will come and worship." This is a "come to us" method of ministry and a perspective reminiscent of the Kevin Costner movie, *Field of Dreams*, "If you build it, they will come." The church expects outsiders to leave their turf and meet God on the official church location's turf. Leading missional scholars, Alan Roxburgh and M. Scott Boren, observe that even though the church in America is living in a "pluralized and globalized" culture, "most churches operate with structures designed for a time when church was firmly at the center."[40] This view perceives that outsiders will be drawn to worship at a permanent building formally consecrated and functioning as a place where God resides and waits to bless them.

The posture of luring drivers from the freeway into the church building to find God is a centripetal (inward focus) posture that hails from Christendom, a time during which the established church still held a position of great influence in society. Christendom hails from Emperor Constantine in the fourth century, who made Christianity the official state religion in the Roman Empire. This led to the ideology of the church

---

40. Alan Roxburgh and M. Scott Boren, *Introducing the Missional Church: What It Is, Why it Matters, How to Become One* (Grand Rapids: Baker Books, 2009), 80.

holding a central, powerful, and influential position, which is also referred to as Constantinianism. The era of Constantine became the epitome of Christian dominance in culture, the impact of which continues to reverberate to the present. Even though he ruled centuries ago, Constantine's dominance had such a remarkable impact on Christianity that its effects still linger today. During his time, citizens were born into the church and evangelism was unnecessary since virtually the entire culture had religious affiliation. Even though in some parts of society the church still holds significant influence, most public sectors in metropolitan areas are becoming increasingly secular, with sprawling educational, governmental, and hospital systems.

For this reason, the belief that "people will come to [the building] to meet God and find fellowship with others"[41] is no longer a viable evangelism strategy in a post-Christendom world. This posture is attractional, which is the opposite of missional, because it waits passively for outsiders to come to the church instead of engaging people where they are. Instead of the church seeking out the unchurched, the unchurched must seek out the church on their turf. This mentality is inherent in a "come to us" posture of ministry where outsiders take the initiative of crossing borders to get to the church. The unchurched become the missionaries crossing into unfamiliar religious territory and adopting the "Christianized culture." On one occasion, the church board decided they needed to reach a broader range of people, especially the growing Muslim community in the neighborhood. The changing demographic in the area caused them to acquire a sign inviting passers-by to worship, which included Muslims. It was their expectation that a sign inviting Muslims should produce results and they would see this people group walk into the sanctuary to worship the Christian God. Sticking up a sign inviting Muslims was their idea of being an inclusive church reaching out to the nations.

A "come to us" posture is in stark contrast to a "go to them" strategy of evangelism that springs from an incarnational impulse. This outward orientation seeks to engage outsiders in their communities. The church

---

41. Frost and Hirsch, *The Shaping of Things to Come*, 18.

builds relationships with others without the preoccupation of getting them into the church. If neighborhood residents decide on joining the church, it is the icing on the cake. Drawing community residents to make them faithful church members, however, is not the primary motivator since attendance does not guarantee that a follower of Christ is being formed. This "go to them" strategy genuinely desires relationships and seeks to tear down walls of separation without any underlying agenda except a desire to see others grow in their relationships with Christ. Members foster relationships and build bridges in their own neighborhoods and workplaces only to represent Christ and share his love and grace, exhibited mainly through their lives and the gospel message.

It is possible that the closest a person will ever get to church is through the interactions they have with a believer outside of the church location. Once trust has been established, he or she may agree to participate in a home gathering in the neighborhood rather than in the church building. The unchurched will sense a believer's disingenuous motives when the primary goal is to get the unchurched to cross the border from the secular to the religious zone. If it does occur, it should happen naturally. Asking outsiders if they would like to attend church should be initiated with wisdom and patience.

SELF-SERVING

When worship and God's presence are confined to a geographic location, it is easy for that church to become self-serving. Sustaining the operating costs of the church requires the seats to be filled and growth to be measured both by people attending services and structural expansion. The resources of the church are spent trying to get people into the building during one of the scheduled service hours or special events. The church looks to extract the unchurched from their communities, further isolating them from their spheres of influence. Emerging church leaders Gibbs and Bolger encourage the church not to "occupy a reactive and defensive stance in regard to culture but rather seek to engage it as insiders."[42] An

---

42. Gibbs and Bolger, *Emerging Churches*, 75.

incarnational approach, however, requires "the church to find ways to engage its community that build relationships" and "to truly be present in the community, to live with the people it is called to serve."[43] When the church expects outsiders to take the initiative and seek the church on its own terms, it is being served rather than serving the community.

THE LORD'S HOUSE

Today, some church leaders promote the importance of coming to church because it is the "Lord's house," subtly inferring that his presence is confined to a place, especially their own building. Jesus responded to the Pharisees, saying, "the Kingdom of God is within you" (Lk. 17:21), and warned his disciples to be cautious when people claim to have God figured out, saying, "'Look here!' or 'Look there!'" (Lk. 17:23). This should be an encouragement to ordinary believers. The Kingdom of God is made manifest through the members of the body as they engage the world. Attractional churches have a permanent and established building for worship and sometimes attempt to localize God's presence as a marketing strategy to attract people to their services or events. They promote their geographic location as an official worship center where God can be found, as if it were the main place where his presence resides.

This dynamic is like the Old Testament Temple in Jerusalem, where God's presence made its dwelling in the Holy of Holies, making it the official sacred site to find fellowship with God. In today's version, the local church becomes the exclusive venue for an encounter with God. Like the ancient priests, the pastor is the mediator, possessing special access to the divine. This creates an elitist environment where the pastor is placed on a pedestal and becomes a "favored" servant of the Lord, while everyone else has limited access to God's throne. The pastor has a "special" relationship with the Lord in comparison to the sub-par connection of most of the members. This elevates the status of credentialed minsters and places them on a pedestal. Localizing God's presence to a physical church and

---

43. Beach, *The Church in Exile*, 2860, Kindle.

elevating certain ministers over others creates a wide clergy-laity divide that has consumeristic roots at its core.

CONSUMERISM IN THE CHURCH

Consumerism is a business-oriented, supply-and-demand system in American society that has infiltrated the attractional church model. This system is described by Soong-Chan Rah, "Social life is reduced to the exchange of goods and products and human life is reduced to a consumable value based upon material worth above and beyond any spiritual worth."[44] In other words, humans become objects and their worth is based on their usefulness and benefit in achieving a goal or financial benchmark. Michael Frost adds, "We are treating people like a market, seeing them as clientele, not image-bearers of the living God."[45] Individuals become tools to be utilized to help achieve the church's goals and objectives.

Pointing outsiders to a building and stating that God can be found inside is only the initial strategy that attractional churches utilize to gain adherents. Once inside, worshippers are constantly being targeted to attend paid seminars, workshops, and retreats. They are bombarded with events and conferences where nationally recognized speakers are enlisted to rally the support and involvement of local congregations. Often, through these various venues, access to special knowledge through divine revelation and special access to the supernatural are promoted as a marketing ploy to enhance excitement and participation. Moreover, members are asked to give financially or volunteer to staff a barrage of projects and activities, keeping them busy and engaged in its internal life. Commitment to Christ becomes involvement in the milieu of activities along with their financial contributions. Members of congregations become the target of the plethora of products and services offered within the "Christianese culture." In the end, members are poorer, more tired, and confused. They are pulled in multiple directions so the "sages" that are on stage can gain increased notoriety and acclamation.

---

44. Rah, *The Next Evangelicalism*, 448, Kindle.
45. Michael Frost, *The Road to Missional*, 66.

One of the detriments of the attractional posture is that it has been influenced largely by American consumerism in its way of measuring success. Rah stipulates that many pastors measure success by "the numerical size of the church and the financial health of the church."[46] The attractional church measures its success by the three Bs: budget, butts, and building. This standard of success is more in line with Fortune 500 companies than what the church should be focused on. Ministries influenced by corporate America apply formulas and techniques to grow their churches and increase the bottom line. In a capitalist church, "the primary indicator of God's blessing is bigger and bigger congregations irrespective of the missional quality of those congregations,"[47] asserts Frost.

Consumerism causes an obsession with the numerical and structural expansion of the church. The size of the congregation with its corresponding visible manifestation becomes evidence that God's favor is being poured out. The suffering servant image, with which many Christians would identify Jesus, becomes Christ depicted as sitting on a golden throne, much like a Roman emperor. Instead of embodying the humble servant, Jesus is now hailed as a cultural hero, conquering poverty and amassing territory to build his Kingdom with material prosperity. The resources to expand the sprawling architectural structures of church "campuses" is off the backs of the members. Instead, the church needs to heed the words of Jesus, "For where your treasure is, there your heart will be also" (Mt. 6:21). Success in consumeristic ministries mirrors the corporate world's definition of success. Corporations define success as growing their bottom line by amassing equity and assets. The way companies grow their bottom line is by persuading more customers to buy their products. In an attractional church, the products and services that attendees are buying are worship services, programs and activities, seminars, books, and so on in exchange for their time, energy, and finances. Churches use similar marketing and advertising strategies to try to lure prospective customers into their spiritual retail store.

---

46. Rah, *The Next Evangelicalism*, 533, Kindle.
47. Frost, *The Road to Missional*, 72.

Following the corporate model, attractional churches set similar year-end financial projections, and the pastor has expectations to meet certain benchmarks, just like CEOs. Pastors who reach their goals and projections achieve higher job security, just like a CEO who increases the company's stock value on Wall Street. Building on this premise, Eugene Peterson tweeted, "The vocation of pastor has been replaced by the strategies of religious entrepreneurs with business plans."[48] The church is not a corporation, and its success and the way it operates should not be measured by the same criteria as corporate America. Numerical and physical expansion should not be the focal point but rather faithfulness to God's call, even when it does not increase the bottom line or expand the church's real estate acquisitions. The church is called to be faithful to the leading of the Lord. The attractional church idolizes the dollar and sees members as resources to be used. The consumeristic church assumes that "all church growth, in terms of membership and finances, is always good, no matter the cost,"[49] in the words of Frost.

The church should not have as priority the same values that American capitalism possesses. The attractional church focuses on the profits and losses associated with operating and maintaining a central and established worship site. Outreach ministries find their main objective in attracting attendees. Consumerism's allegiance is centered on production and prioritizes—"size, power, and achievement."[50] The attractional church falsely sees the reign of God as expanding the membership, structure, and economic success of the organization. A primary focus on internal needs yields a tendency to retain individuals, since they provide the resources that make the church machine run. This has an isolating effect on members, further distancing them from their own contexts and ultimately making them absent to their own neighbors.

---

48. Eugene Peterson, Twitter (Oct. 27, 2014), accessed November 22, 2016, https://twitter.com/petersondaily/status/526896657926217728.
49. Frost, *The Road to Missional: Journey to the Center of the Church* (Baker Books: Grand Rapids, MI, 2011), 73.
50. Frost, *The Road to Missional: Journey to the Center of the Church*, 72.

Instead, the church could harness an outward thrust, recognizing the importance of equipping and supporting its members to be missionaries, and equipping them to live incarnationally in society, especially during times in which the general population is not seeking out the church on its own initiative. This type of church seeks to "go" make disciples and to be the church in their neighborhoods and workplaces, which are the hardest-to-reach spheres in an increasingly post-church culture. An outward thrust causes the central and established worship site to be less of a factor and moved from the center of religious life. When the church gathers, it is to encourage, equip, and empower members to be missionaries the rest of the week, in areas where the unchurched live. What the building looks like and what amenities it offers become less important because attendees know that their mission field is outside the four walls. If members' lives are absorbed by their churches, how will they share their lives and the gospel?

A Church Fundraiser

When the church becomes an established, central, and permanent worship site focused on its material needs, there can be a drift toward seeing the local community as a resource that can contribute toward meeting their financial obligations. Instead of the church serving the community and attempting to represent Christ well by addressing needs, the roles are reversed. Now the community is the one that is enlisted to help support the survival of the church. One such church holds a community fundraiser every year to fill the financial deficiencies to meet all the operating costs of having an established building. The annual fundraiser seeks to attract the community to the event where there is an auction, a live band, games, food, and fun activities. Local businesses are solicited to donate auction items toward the cause. In the end, the focus is on whether the church can meet its fundraising goals.

In the above case, it appears as if sharing the love of Christ in word and deed was overshadowed by internal concerns. The community was serving the church instead of the church serving the community. Additionally, the church's fundraising event competed with another community fundraiser that sought to raise support for the financial gaps in the local school system. The church's fundraiser potentially could have taken away funds from the other event. Over the last ten years, the church had been in decline, leaving the aging congregation unable to pay the operating costs of sustaining the maintenance of the building, the pastor's salary and benefits, and its various programs. In the most recent year, the church paid $10,000 to upgrade their sign, needed an additional $25,000 to pave the parking lot, and received a $2,500 estimate to fix the roof leak in the gym. Church leadership still perceived that the cause for their declining numbers was that the church building was not "attractive" enough, so they tasked the community with their survival. The congregation did not seem to be impacting the community in any way but was relying on the cooperation of its residents to meet its expenditures. The board spent countless hours obsessing over the building and arguing about the funds needed to complete the proposed projects.

The Building is the Mission

When the energy of the church is directed inward, management and maintenance become the primary task of the leadership, eclipsing the church's mission in the world. Churches use capitalistic models for measuring success, which Soong-Chan Rah describes as an absorption with "the numerical size of the church and the financial health of the church (oftentimes reflected in the condition and appearance of the church building)."[51] Even in their architecture, some churches are reconciling faith with consumeristic inspiration. Rah describes this phenomenon as, "Our movie theater sanctuaries (to appease the consumer looking for an hour's worth of entertainment on a Sunday morning) and our mall-like church buildings reveal our captivity to the materialistic and consumeristic culture of American society."[52] The church becomes excessively concerned over protecting and preserving its material well-being that this becomes its mission. Any outreach in the community is driven by the church's own needs and less on participating with God and seeing the Kingdom expand outwardly.

---

51. Soong-Chan Rah, *The Next Evangelicalism: Freeing the Church from Western Cultural Captivity* (Downers Grove: Intervarsity, 2009), 534, Kindle.
52. Ibid., 492, Kindle.

CAROL'S YOUNG ADULTS GROUP

Carol was a teacher who had been in the public school system for twenty-five years. Teaching was her calling and she supernaturally connected with young people. She showed devotion to her students and genuine interest to see them thrive and reach their full potential. She had an incredible impact on her students, instilling in them a desire to achieve their best, and many kept in touch with her even after graduating from high school. Some of her students had such admiration toward her that they would stop by her house to ask her for advice on difficult decisions. Eventually, she felt led to host a young adult's Bible study in her home and had 15-20 students on average attend weekly. This was incarnational ministry at its finest. Being incarnational "assumes that God is already at work in the world" and means "stepping into what God is doing and remaining faithful to that calling."[53]

Word of this group got to the elders of Carol's church. They chided her for not letting the leadership know sooner about this group so she could have proper covering from the church. Carol's church was affiliated with an established denomination and had an officially sanctioned congregation. Since Carol was a member, the church felt they needed to have a representative from the church to monitor the study for accountability purposes. Carol had her membership at this congregation, so the elders felt they had to supervise the study, giving Carol the proper authority to carry out an outreach of this type that was not conducted on church grounds. Carol was an indigenous leader who saw God working right where she lived in the lives of the people with whom she interacted through natural encounters throughout the week. In her view, she was simply yielding to the move of the Spirit in her life. She saw a need in her community, and God was the one who was drawing youngsters to her weekly gathering.

Gradually, some of the leadership at her church attempted to get her group to assimilate into the church body and get more involved with congregational life. These young adults would repeatedly get invites to

---

53. Frost, *The Road to Missional*, 131.

attend scheduled services and were enticed with special guest speakers on certain occasions. They figured that meeting in such an informal setting in Carol's living room was only a stepping stone and a primer to get them ready for "real" church experience conducted in the traditional manner. The church had experienced some decline in recent years, especially with the younger demographic. They were longing to get back to the glory days where the sanctuary would be packed with young people on Sunday mornings.

An elder of the church perceived this group to be the answer to prayer since they had been asking for a rise in membership. They were desperately seeking ways to increase attendance and to get back to their growing ways. The church had been looking to grow the young adult's ministry specifically but had struggled to reach this age range more than any other group. They saw potential in Carol's group to fill this gap, but there was hesitation on behalf of the students. The majority were not interested in joining the established, programmed church. They had not signed up for that and felt they were part of a church already, which was their weekly gathering at Carol's house. Most had some previous affiliation in a traditional church setting but had been disconnected in recent years from a church body. They seemed content with the group that had developed at Carol's house.

The students expressed being comfortable meeting in a more informal setting because they felt freer to be themselves. Additionally, according to Alan J. Roxburgh and Fred Romanuk, young people in general "are not shaped by loyalty to institutions and have little interest in joining church groups and programs."[54] Since this group did not transition toward becoming participatory members of the official, sanctioned church, they were seen as a rogue outfit. What followed was an uncomfortable tension between Carol and a few of the elders when she attended church on Sunday mornings. She did not feel it was right to pressure her students to become members of the church. Instead, she allowed them to make their own decisions without interfering This initiative should have produced

---

54. Alan J. Roxburgh and Fred Romanuk, *The Missional Leader: Equipping Your Church to Reach a Changing World* (San Francisco: Jossey-Bass, 2006), 23.

praise and joy in her church, knowing that young people in the community were being reached and progress was being made in their spiritual walk. Her church needed to understand that younger, postmodern groups "are not turning to institutional, traditional church as part of their spiritual journey."[55]

Naturally Forming Groups

Carol's young adult's group was born naturally without any church planting strategies or methods. It was through caring relationships that she connected to these young people, and they were growing by leaps and bounds. She was not seeking for them to become members, to volunteer, or to give a tithe. She was simply interested in their well-being and genuinely had their best interests in mind. She felt there were many students who were disoriented with life and needing to belong to a support group. After some time, on their own initiative and without any prompting, they contributed by bringing food and asking for donations to help Carol buy groceries. They also supported one another whenever someone in the group was going through difficulty. On one occasion, a young man's car broke down on his way to work. After paying for the car repairs, he had no money left for his rent. The group united in initiating a fundraising event to help him pay his rent for the month. They prayed and sought God's guidance regarding how to help individuals in and outside the group who needed assistance.

The local church's interest in the group ended when they did not seem to be moving toward becoming affiliated with the congregation. After five years of gathering at Carol's house, this group dissolved as they married and started their own families and moved for employment purposes. One of the advantages of this kind of organic, natural-forming communities, such as Carol initiated, is that they do not have to last forever since they are not gathering in a permanent building. Reggie McNeal would describe this group as a missional community because they "have no buildings to maintain and, in many cases, no

---

55. McNeal, *Missional Communities*, 8.

clergy to support."[56] They can be flexible and mobile and adapt to the ever-changing needs of the people without trying to force ministry to happen.

For five years, Carol's group was active and served their spiritual and physical needs for that moment in time. Once that purpose was met, they moved to the next stage of life, taking with them the solid biblical foundation which had been laid by Carol. They were better prepared to face their futures and foster deeper relationships with the Lord. This group was a seasonal outreach that was not intended to be an established and permanent worship site to exist in perpetuity. It served the needs of the group for that time and there was no pressure to keep it going after its purpose was served. Carol did not feel a financial burden because her house was paid for. She also did not have to burden the young adults with some of the costs that are required to operate an established worship location. Maintaining this group did not require vast resources, so Carol never had to burden the group with expenses, and she could freely give of her life without expecting any financial compensation. She welcomed any contributions that were earmarked for the benefit of the group, especially since she provided a weekly meal, the cost of which added up over time. But this cost was minimal in contrast to a permanent building that requires extensive support and resources to keep it afloat.

Servant Leadership

Carol was a gifted teacher and had the personality, education, and experience to properly serve this group. Yet she was looked down on by her church and seen as not meeting the institutional requirements that would give her legitimacy. She had not gone through a formal ordination process sanctioned by her church, nor did she possess an official certificate by a denominational body to give her proper authority to minister to others. Moreover, she did not have an official position at her church, which caused the elders to question her spiritual fitness to serve the group. It is important to note that it was not through a position or title that Carol gained

---

56. McNeal, *Missional Communities*, xx.

the respect and adoration of these young adults. Instead, she won them over by giving of her life to them. This is not to say that leaders should not pursue credentialing, but even officially sanctioning a minister will not necessarily make him or her successful or fit to lead others.

While most pursue credentials for the right reasons, some inevitably are motivated by desires for recognition, legitimacy, and authority. Denominations tend to give licensed ministers special status by reserving seats of honor at church meetings and events. They are often invited to attend conferences and meetings, excluding others who have not attained proper licensing. Unfortunately, this invokes a culture that treats those who are not licensed as second-class servants, without taking into consideration their Christ-like character. For Carol's young adults, it made no difference whether she was licensed. It was the love and care that they received from her that caused them to respond. Jesus exemplified such a servant posture of leadership by washing his disciples' feet and saying to them, "Whoever wants to be great among you must serve the rest of you like a servant" (Mk 10:43). While Carol had little experience in managing programs or preparing church services, , she exhibited a deep love for God and neighbor, as well as a listening spirit to recognize how Christ was at work.

Instead of attempting to assert control, the established church might consider approaching a missional community like the one Carol led with a humble and service-oriented posture. Instead of undermining her giftedness, they could have sought to help and support Carol, who was reaching her community. The church needed to affirm Carol's gifts, provide counsel when necessary, and become a source of empowerment. Her church leadership would have done well to be ready to assist her in any way she needed. Instead of looking down on her and looking to see how the church could benefit from her work, church leaders should have set aside any agenda that was self-seeking. The leadership of Carol's established church had ulterior motives. Their agenda was selfish and their aim was, primarily, to see her group transition over to the central worship site, where they could assimilate them into the programs and activities of the church.

Church leaders were hoping that these young people could be molded into good members. Having the group assimilate to the centralized location would allow the church to maintain some sense of control over them, and they might revitalize the young adult ministry that had experienced severe decline in the last decade.

This group had a shepherd and they knew her voice when she called out to them. Her name was Carol, and these students continue to stay in touch with her, knowing she genuinely cared for them and was always available to talk through issues with them.

Partnerships

The leadership of the church needed to understand that the reason these young adults were attending Carol's home group was because it was not conducted in a traditional way. Their gathering incorporated essential elements in worship like prayer, Bible study, testimonies, dialogue, and other practices to create Christ-followers. Additionally, they felt they had found a community to which they belonged. In the words of missionaries Anita and John Koeshall, "A healthy student ministry should be recognized as a member-church"[57] and not viewed as lesser than the typical paradigm. Jesus said, "Nor do they put new wine into old wineskins, or else the wineskins break, the wine is spilled, and the wineskins are ruined. But they put new wine into new wineskins, and both are preserved" (Mt. 9:17). What this group had going worked well. People, who are accustomed to a more traditional style, need to be careful not to impose their preconceived notions of church on others. Trying to force this young gathering into an "old wineskin" could have had disastrous effects, possibly even causing what had been thriving to disintegrate.

Even though this group did not fit the typical paradigm, it should not have been dismissed as a lesser community of faith when compared to the more traditional congregation. Carol was not against church membership, but she felt they needed to make that decision for themselves. Her group

---

57. Anita and John Koeshall, "Images of a Missiological Ecclesiology," Lecture series presented at AGTS (Springfield, MO: Fall 2010), J. Philip Hogan World Missions Series Monograph, Vol. V, 42.

had all the attributes necessary to be considered a healthy young adult ministry. Everything a traditional church could experience was taking place in their group but in a way to which they could relate. The gospel message was simply packaged differently than the traditional model. Yet there was a misconception that this group was not receiving the message of the gospel because they were worshipping in a manner different from the attractional way. Church members perceived that proper worship required an official building with all its trappings like a pulpit, pews, stage, and so on. The gospel message did not change—only the context in which it was delivered was different. Carol had provided an informal and relaxed venue for them to grow in Christ—what mattered was that they received the gospel message.

These young people experienced accelerated growth; they participated, shaped, and contributed to the group. They prayed earnestly, reading and meditating on the Scriptures, and supported one another with the challenges of life. The leadership responsibilities in local churches are usually given to the pastor and elders who perform most of the spiritual duties. The attractional church falsely perceives itself to be the primary tool of God's mission and the focal point of religious life. Yet Carol was a "person of peace" and an extension of the local church. The tentacles of her church were reaching out through her into the broader community. The established leadership more than likely would have never reached this particular group. They did not have the rapport or influence that Carol had established with these students. They also did not have the history that Carol had when she taught many of them in high school. Hers was an "indigenous tribe" that had sprung up and provided what they needed for fellowship and discipleship.

In Carol's case, her church had an image of what they wanted this young adult ministry to look like, but the church's vision was interfering with the work that was being accomplished in the neighborhood. When the institutional church becomes the only legitimate expression of the Kingdom in the world, they become like the Star Trek "Borg," assimilating and extracting individuals from their communities to join the church (the mother ship) with the hope of making them faithful members. This causes the reach of the local church to shrink and hinders people like Carol from becoming salt and light in their own contexts. Instead, local churches should encourage and support this kind of community outreach with no strings attached. Such a posture would broaden the reach of the church to the surrounding neighborhoods where the unchurched live. The local church leadership should also attempt to understand the perspectives of a different generation and the different set of challenges they face. Through servant leadership, instead of controlling leadership, the local church can begin to build trust with the disenfranchised. The community needs to see a genuine and loving congregation that is not self-seeking. When the church focuses on the wrong things, people become objects to accomplish real or perceived goals and objectives.

Established and Permanent

> They refer to the building as the "sanctuary." They try to encourage the faithful to revere their sanctuary in the same way that Israel revered their temple. Indeed, this is the same way that many religious communities revere their holy places of worship, whether mosques, temples, wats, shrines, basilicas, or cathedrals. But in instituting his mission through the sending out of the seventy-two, Jesus implies a complete and utter worldview shift. Now, every household, every village, every town and city is the dwelling place of God.[58]

Members of officially sanctioned, attractional churches can mistakenly possess a mental model that assumes that a structure is the primary indicator of legitimacy and the pinnacle for an encounter with the divine. The building becomes the visible manifestation of God's presence so the church feels its appearance should be grander and more impressive than ordinary spaces. Even though the first-century church gathered primarily in homes until domesticated, non-traditional spaces like Carol's living

---

58. Frost, *The Road to Missional*, 117.

room today are considered spiritually inferior. When ministries start in informal settings and gain momentum, some believe that the next step is to move into an established and official worship site with corresponding structural expansion to accommodate the growth. Some leaders who start naturally forming, grassroots movements hope to eventually transition into formal locations fitted with a church sign, stage, pews, and other elements that make it official. Once all these elements are in place, it becomes "The House of the Lord." The building becomes a symbol of permanence and stability, giving the allusion of legitimacy as the dwelling place of God. The group leader's official status is confirmed through his or her ability to acquire a designated worship location. With a building and a pulpit for addressing the congregation, he or she has attained the status necessary to be called a "lead pastor."

There is a misconception that to be legitimate, pastors and ministers serve exclusively in an official location complete with a parking lot, a sanctuary, and Sunday school rooms. Additionally, if a pastor is not behind a pulpit preaching to a congregation, accompanied by a dynamic praise and worship team, their ministries are not taken as seriously as those who serve in more informal settings. Indeed, they tend to be lumped together with other unofficial efforts like Carol's. Unless the pastor has a designated location exclusively for worship and a reasonable number of attendees, he or she is considered second-level. Some gatherings may even be considered rogue and untamable, perceived as splitting from the establishment, especially if the faith community is meeting in a third space not properly constituted as a religious building by a denominational body.

THE OFFICIAL LOCATION

Any attempt to worship or serve God outside of the officially sanctioned building during one of the scheduled service hours is cast as inferior or secondary to the main gathering on Sunday morning. The church becomes the "official" location rather than the gathered people of God. People believe that to experience God's presence at its full potential, it is necessary to go to "God's House" because that is where he manifests himself more than any other place. Members are enculturated to believe that the presence of God cannot be experienced fully unless it occurs at the official worship center on Sunday mornings. Attempts to reach outsiders in the community through informal gatherings and celebrations are considered inferior or distractions to the "real" experience on Sunday morning.

The truth is that living life with people in our communities and workplaces is the avenue where the church can have the greatest impact toward the unchurched and society at large. If the church is isolated and disconnected from their neighborhoods, these neighborhoods will not be reached. It is through the daily and ordinary interactions like inviting our neighbors for dinner, attending a child's birthday party, or being a friend to someone going through a divorce that makes manifest the presence of God.

INSTITUTIONAL LEADERSHIP

Leaders who have positions in established institutions often feel their positions alone should generate reverence from others. There is a misconception that the unchurched still hold clergy in high esteem and will seek the counsel of a local pastor for their life dilemmas. Also, institutional leaders tend to "focus first on the stability and well-being of the institution, than on the church's mission in the world."[59] Since the institutions they serve provide these leaders with legitimacy and financial benefit, this gain, for which they have worked so hard, may cause them to seek the best interest of the institution first and the mission of God second. Their focus can favor institutional success, which is usually propagating the hierarchal structure that has given their life meaning and purpose. Clergy feel forced to perpetuate the religious system for fear of losing the platform which is giving them institutional legitimacy and authority. Without this platform, they would lose their standing within the system. If they spent significant time jumping through the hoops necessary to become ordained through the institution, they are compelled to "prop-it-up" in order to get a return on their investment.

---

59. Callahan, *Effective Church Leadership*, 82.

Even during a time when mainline religious institutions are losing their societal authority and prestige in America, they seem to be holding on for dear life to maintain the structures that legitimize their existence. These power structures continue to fight for control and survival, even in an era where the established church is increasingly marginalized and pushed further from the center of society. These hierarchal systems still expect to have a certain level of influence over religion in society. But, in fact, they have become irrelevant to many postmoderns, who prefer a flattened hierarchal structure which is more collaborative and flexible.

Instead of fighting for the little bit of territory they have left, these institutions should reverse course to support and partner with more decentralized forms of community like the one Carol started. Instead of seeing such groups as adversaries and competitors, the established church should support and empower these grassroots movements and see themselves as being on the same team. The younger generations are suspicious of established, top-down, religious systems. They value egalitarian and participatory forms of community. Their motivations for being in community are to have a place to belong, to find meaning, and to seek answers to life's questions in informal settings among trusted friends. Especially when a younger person is looking for an alternative to "mainline" churches, missional leaders in the trenches of society will be necessary to guide these individuals toward growth in Christ. Leaders with a solid theological Christian grounding, journeying side-by-side with these "spiritual nomads," will keep them from getting lost in today's pluralistic maze.

Top-Down Leadership

Inherent in Christendom is a mindset that tends to favor hierarchal, centralized, and inflexible patterns of leadership. This term "Christendom" is derived from the era of Emperor Constantine, who gave birth to the movement and instituted a new, top-down system in which "clergy gained privileges and alone performed functions once the task of all Christians,"[60]

---

60. Stuart Murray, *Post Christendom: Church and Mission in a Strange World* (Waynesboro, GA: Paternoster, 2004), 125.

and "clergy performed services, taking charge of more and more of the liturgy until the laity became almost passive."[61] This original hierarchy placed clergy on pedestals and gave them seats of honor at various religious as well as political functions. Like Constantine's model, most American churches today also have patterns, traditions, and ideologies that set a distinction between the few called to ministry and the majority who function passively. The involvement of the laity in spiritual matters is primarily supporting the vision of the pastor. There continues to be a distinction between those who have a "higher" calling to be pastors and leaders and laity who do not.

Regarding the effects of the clergy and laity divide, Bosch writes, "For almost nineteen centuries and in virtually all ecclesiastical traditions, ministry has been understood almost exclusively in terms of the service of ordained ministers."[62] Since he called a mix of different kinds of people, such as fisherman, tax collectors, and even religious leaders, Jesus's selection of his disciples was contrary to the exclusive call from a priestly class. He called his disciples to follow him (Mk. 1:20), not a hierarchal, ecclesiastical system. Regardless of who they were and what position in society they held, Jesus invited individuals from diverse backgrounds to a life dedicated to following him.

The laity typically populate a void of authority or expertise necessary to perform ministerial functions. Even though Constantine's rule took place hundreds of years ago and is a bygone era in history, remnants persist among church leaders that still resemble this model. A sort of caste system in leadership has kept ordinary believers underdeveloped, relying on the clergy to perform most of religious duties and services. The clergy are called into ministry, while the laity are the ordinary and untrained believers, tasked with supporting the professional ministers in their churches. The support usually comes in the form of providing time and money for the church's inward needs. A culture of dependency is

---

61. Ibid., 126.
62. Bosch, *Transforming Mission*, 467.

created when the few are responsible for most of the spiritual functions in a local church.

Instead, an inverse of this culture needs to be developed—that of raising and equipping local missionaries and not relegating the bulk of religious functions to a few professional ministers. Those tasked with leading local churches should empower the members of the body to participate in God's mission. The gift of leadership (e.g., Rom. 12:8) bestowed by the Spirit is not to control or monopolize ministry, but rather to nourish participation from the whole community. With a collaborative approach, multiplicities of gifts are then made available to the body for the sake of God's mission in the world.

In attractional churches, the "caste system" that is fostered resembles an ancient paradigm within the local church that separates Christians into two groups—the clergy and laity. The clergy are called into ministry, while the laity are the ordinary and untrained believers tasked with supporting the professional ministers in their churches. This type of church will have limited impact in surrounding communities because the minister stays inside a consecrated building performing spiritual functions. Missional leadership, on the other hand, empowers the members of the body to participate in God's mission outside the walls of the church. When the entire body of Christ is thus empowered, members will become missionaries in the spheres where they live and work.

Closing Thoughts

The church has difficulty seeing beyond itself when the central worship site becomes the focal point and center of religious life. An inward focus causes the church to forget about the greater mission of God and how they are to go and serve their communities. The church becomes too preoccupied with laying up treasures for themselves and they forget the true heart of God. Jesus said, "I did not come to be served, but to serve and give my life as a ransom for many" (Mt 20:28). Too often, the local church expects the community to serve its internal needs instead of the church serving the needs of the community.

The consumerism that is prevalent in American society has heavily influenced the church to the degree that people are reduced to a commodity. As Rah states, "An individual's worth in society is based upon what assets they bring and what possessions they own."[63] One of the byproducts of attractionalism is that people are the players that allow the church to achieve its goals and objectives. Preoccupation with attractionalism causes the church to see individuals as consumers, some moving the needle more than others. Success is measured by the growth and expansion of the church, and this kind of preoccupation blinds it to the external needs in the community.

BIBLICAL INSIGHTS

In the Old Testament, biblical scholar Lee Beach claims that Israel's primary strategy for mission was through giving "testimony to the greatness of Yahweh through its internal life as a nation" and "worshiping and practicing the law faithfully."[64] This strategy looked to draw and lure other nations to Jerusalem, the Israel's center for worship and religious practice. This mindset used attraction as the main strategy in drawing others to worship where God could be found. The posture was heavily reliant on a "come to us" mentality, with the expectation that if it were built, people would come and offer their devotion. "The Jerusalem temple was the place where Israel believed God's presence was particularly immediate,"[65] notes Beach. If the same centripetal thrust had been used in the first-century church after Jesus's ascension, the gospel message would have been hindered from reaching the nations since an emphasis on "gathering" would have superseded a "scattering" of the church.

Under the Holy Spirit's direction, the New Testament church instead adopted a "centrifugal" posture, which Beach describes as including an "outward thrust that takes seriously the missional nature

---

63. Beach, *The Church in Exile*, 445, Kindle.
64. Ibid., 2895, Kindle.
65. Beach, *The Church in Exile*, 675, Kindle.

of God's people and Christ's call for his church to be a people who go into the world."[66] Emerging church scholars Gibbs and Bolger write, "We are commanded by Christ as his followers to live incarnationally, to overcome boundaries, to express the God-life, and to recognize where God is at work in every realm."[67] In moving toward becoming missional, the church should not be exclusively inward, focusing entirely on the internal life of the Christian community. The church is not a place, but the living temple of God in which the Holy Spirit dwells. The Holy Spirit now empowers and sends the church to continue Jesus's mission to the ends of the earth. In the act of going, the church leaves its comfort and security so it can be a blessing to the nations, locally or globally. Jesus left his heavenly realm, seated at the right hand of the Father, becoming a mere mortal. It was through his vulnerability that he brought salvation to the world. Now, the church goes forward in his power, leaving their comfort and security, to make him known.

WORDS AND PHRASES TO REMEMBER

1. **Centripetal Church:** The momentum and energy is primarily inward. When taken to the extreme, the church becomes self-serving and blind to the community it is called to serve. Its focus turns to its internal needs.
2. **Decentralized Movement:** The physical location for gathering and worship is less of a priority than relationships and community-building. This church is fluid and mobile. It can adapt to its circumstances freely as challenges and opportunities present themselves. Even without an official location, the church would continue to function since the building is not the glue that holds the congregation together.

---

66. Ibid., 2900, Kindle.
67. Gibbs and Bolger, *Emerging Churches*, 75.

3. **Centralized Worship Site:** A permanent and established location for fellowship and service. The worship site becomes the symbol of God's presence like the Temple model of the Old Testament. His presence is localized to a specific place and this location becomes the center for spiritual practices. Any worship outside of this location is deemed inferior.
4. **Church Consumerism:** The value of individuals based on their ability to help achieve the church's material and financial goals. The church takes on a capitalistic ideology and sees people's worth as their usefulness to helping them achieve their expansion projects.

KEY VERSES TO REFLECT

Acts 7:48
Luke 17:21
Matthew 6:21

DISCOVERY QUESTIONS

1. How would you describe the difference between a "come to us" versus a "go to them" model of ministry?

2. In your own words, how does a centripetal church (attractional) become self-serving?

3. What is the difference between institutional (hierarchal) leadership and servant leadership?

4. What Scripture verses speak to you after reading this chapter?

CHAPTER 4

Rethinking Sacred Space

MENTAL MODELS

I attended a conference in January in Minneapolis, Minnesota, after which I decided to visit my wife's family in South Dakota. On my way back to the airport, I was shocked by the outside temperature. It was -15 degrees. I was wearing four layers of clothes but it didn't seem to matter! After I had been on the road for a couple hours and noon was approaching, I decided to stop at a restaurant for lunch. As I sat down, the waitress brought out a glass filled with ice water. Staring at the ice cubes and looking out the window at the blistering cold, I realized that the waitress had developed a "mental model." This waitress had never evaluated or taken the time to reflect on why she was serving water with ice considering the extreme outside temperature. This story illustrates how mental models can become culturally acceptable ways of functioning even when it does not make sense to function in that way. The attractional model has become second nature in many congregations. Thinking outside the typical paradigm can be difficult, especially when it is embedded in the mindset of the leadership. Even when practices do not make sense, the church continues to function without thinking about how they gather and worship.

ONE SIZE FITS ALL

Alan J. Roxburgh describes mental models as "our internal understanding about how things ought to work and the habits and practices we develop over time based on these inner understandings."[68] The church should

---

68. Alan J. Roxburgh, *Missional Map-Making: Skills for Leading in Times of Transition* (San Francisco, Jossey-Bass, 2010), 194.

learn to reevaluate the way it organizes and gathers to see if it makes sense, especially in post-Christendom America. The structures in the church today are under the guise that there is one church model that is recognized as a worship center. According to Anita and John Koeshall, two of the organizational structures that dominate today's church culture are: "1) a place—a building with seats in a row and a podium in front, and 2) a leader-follower structure of pastor over elders over congregation."[69] These narrow models are limiting the creative power of the Spirit to work in each unique context. There should be no preset templates for how the church decides to organize and be the church. A missional community does not subscribe to the one-size-fits-all model. Instead, the soil determines what life it will support, which is influenced and shaped by the people involved and the particular goals and strategies of the missional impetus that gives rise to the community,[70] according to McNeal.

Changing Venues

In Scripture, God had no problem changing venues or methods for how he met his people and had fellowship with them. Through biblical history, God rattled the ingrained mental models of worship, forcing his people to adapt to an ever-changing spiritual climate. This started in the Garden of Eden, changed at Mt. Sinai, then at the Tabernacle in the desert, and again at the established Temple in Jerusalem, which was followed by God leaving the Temple and journeying with Israel into captivity in Babylon. In the New Testament, God's presence is allusive, spontaneous, and dynamic. The Holy Spirit inhabiting the hearts and minds of his children is what comprises the church—not the form, structure, or shape of the venue in which they decide to meet for fellowship and edification. From the gathering during Pentecost to gathering in households, even under intense Roman persecution, God meets his people when his children are gathered together. The message of the Gospel does not change; only the venue in which the message is delivered changes. The church needs to

---

69. Koeshall, "Ecclesiology-To-Go," 15.
70. McNeal, *Missional Communities*, 33.

rethink sacred space and find alternatives to static and centralized spaces for worship.

THE NEW CHURCH PLANT

To define the term "mental model," the proposition I received to join a church planting team provides a helpful insight. I was given literature describing aspects of the envisioned church. The initial step, working toward an eventual launch several months down the road, boiled down to attempting to get seasoned church people to serve on the planting team. The team would apply their experience and understanding of ministry based on an attractional model from the "mother church." These volunteers would fill the various programs and departments of the building-centered church. They would apply the blueprint from their home church into the new plant. The theory was that the recipe from their home church, including the programs and leadership structure, could easily be replicated elsewhere yielding the same results. The reasoning was that if the "secret sauce" of the parent church was copied, they would also achieve the same success. In McNeal's words, this method is "more like franchising or plug-and-play replication."[71]

Everything they would attempt to implement would be consistent and compared to the attractional model from which they came, including all internal activities and programs. The team would consist of individuals who had been "churched" for a long time and had served in one of the internal programs consistently for several years. If a planting pastor is enlisting volunteers who have come out of an attractional church, the product that will result is the same ministry model from which they came.

The team already had preconceived notions of what church should look like. In other words, they already had an attractional mental model ingrained in their minds and they set out to follow the prescribed recipe. The leadership structure would consist of the predictable lead pastor over elders over congregation model. The thrust would be "centripetal," focusing on attracting outsiders to the main focal point during the week, the

---

71. McNeal, *Missional Communities*, 27.

Sunday morning worship service. Their conception of church was that it was a location and something to which people go. The role of the team would be to evangelize the community by bringing people in to worship. Additionally, it nurtured the premise that a building and Sunday morning services were essential markers for it be considered a legitimate expression of church. To meet the financial requirement of an attractional church structure, a robust fundraising program would be required.

NUMERICAL AND STRUCTURAL EXPANSION

Part of the recipe was that churchgoers recruited from the "mother church" would fill the leadership positions to cater to the new attendees during scheduled events and services. Discipleship consisted of enrolling new attendees in a church program. Worshippers were invited to pick from a menu of options. In this model, as the numerical number of attendees grows, there is corresponding growth in the program offered and in the physical structure of the church to accommodate the increase. The growth, of course, causes the financial burden of the church to increase proportionately. After some time, the pastor enthusiastically announced to the team that he had found a commercial space in the area for only $6,000 per month rent. He thought this was a great deal since he was expecting it to be around $8,000-$10,000. Finding an initial resting place, until they outgrew the location, was the first step in their church planting endeavors. They made sure to outfit the new space in the typical seats-in-a-row, facing-the-stage model so they could begin to worship in a manner to which people were accustomed. Churchgoers from the area would be familiar with this kind of setup, therefore, able to assimilate easily into the worship experience.

AN OFFICIAL CHURCH

The mindset within the church planting group from the beginning was that eventually they would be looking to transition into an officially sanctioned church building that would be more credible than their temporary accommodations. It was expected that, in the weeks to follow, the church would transition to having services and fellowship in an established worship site. This has been the typical church-plant progression. The church would incur additional costs to turn this commercial space into an official place to worship, fit with stage lighting, movie theater chairs, staff offices, baptismal pool, and a plethora of other additions needed for legitimacy. The pastor's status as a leader of a legitimate church rests on the ability to have an official site, formally consecrated as a place of worship.

These improvements, of course, would incur thousands of dollars in expenses, ergo, the rigorous fundraising campaign. It seemed as if most of the planning was spent on strategizing how they could acquire more funds to make the plan bloom into fruition. The church planting team's strength and motivation seemed to digress little-by-little. They were feeling more and more tired, poor, and burned out. Most had full-time jobs in addition to being part of the church planting team. The commute was taking a toll on most of them as well. In addition to volunteering time and energy, they were expected to tithe, since, up to this point, they were covering the bulk of the expenses involved with this new church plant until other backers could be recruited. A few of them started to question why they were involved in the first place. Their quality of life drastically spiraled downward—all to help the pastor reach his objective.

Focusing Inwardly

Considering finances alone, much can be discerned about the church planting process. The financial aspect of this church plant is a good example of a church with an internally focused mindset. Most of the energy is inward, seeking to address the operating demands of the church. The fundraising goal for the first year was $240,000, with the same goal for years 2 and 3. Following is the financial breakdown:

- Church costs: $90,000 (pastoral salary, taxes, housing, benefits, medical)
- Facility costs: $80,000 ($6,000 rent a month plus utilities, electricity, insurance, etc.)

- Central costs: $30,000 (ministry budget: retreats, classes, neighborhood groups, administration, programming, media, communication, etc.)
- Launch fund: $30,000 (startup costs, promotion, music equipment, children's curriculum, signage, etc.)
- Mission: $10,000 (3 local ministries, 2 global ministries, church planting)

Approximately 4% of the church budget would be allotted to mission initiatives, while 96% would go to the internal functioning of the church (programs, pastor salary, building, etc.). Of the 96%, almost half would go to the pastor's salary and benefits in his first year. The pastor left his bi-vocational job, continually reminding the team, "Where God guides he provides" and "The laborer is worthy of his wages." It is worth noting that some secular non-profit organizations have these two figures reversed. Non-profits are scrutinized by donors who make sure their donations are not eaten up by operational costs. These donors want to verify that the funds they are giving are used for the causes they want to support. Whenever a small fraction of the budget is allotted to missions, it is a clear indicator that it will be a program-centric church. Though this church needs to be commended for their giving toward missions, it does not change the fact that it is still primarily focused inwardly with its resources. The bulk of its finances go toward operational costs, and only a small portion of the budget is given toward missions. Oftentimes, a portion is allotted to missions to show would-be backers how the church is contributing toward outside initiatives. In this case, the financial breakdown alone clearly shows that it will be an attractional church.

The budget shows that this church will be focused on filling the pews every Sunday because the mortgage, utilities, and salaries will need to be paid without fail. When the financial burden gets too heavy, the leadership predictably transfers the load to the congregants. To meet financial demands, the pastor often discusses tithing. Going to a church that is always asking for money is a way to keep worshippers at bay. The attendees become the means and resource for fulfilling the church's financial goals.

The three-year financial projection can become a burden on the entire team. The pastor's time can potentially be consumed with thoughts about how to raise the operational costs of running this attractional church. Unable to fulfill the financial projections, the pastor may feel like a failure when he falls short of the 3 Bs (building, budget, and butts) projection. In the attractional model, the pastor's gauge in measuring success revolves around fundraising. There is constant pressure to keep the vision alive and the machine running. The anxiety spills over to all who are involved when projections fall short.

Building-Centered

When the energy is directed inward, the question of who is being served must be asked. It is understandable that churches incur operational costs. When the allocated budget is preoccupied primarily with the internal functioning, however, it becomes a self-serving entity. Its mission becomes the internal life of the church. The internally focused church is primarily concerned with its own needs instead of seeking to serve and bless its community. In addition to serving in missions by going on short-term trips overseas, the community in which they are located should become the main mission field.

This church enters the community and becomes a "taker" rather than "giver." The local funds that could potentially be utilized to address the neglect in the community are further absorbed by the attractional church. The internal needs of the church take precedence over anything externally that does not directly benefit their cause. If, from the beginning, the focus starts with internal needs of the church and less about the needs of the community, the natural progression is for it to become an attractional church. Especially in low-income communities, the attractional church becomes the most well-maintained structure in the entire neighborhood, while the schools, parks, libraries, clinics, and housing units are falling apart. In one example, a church fittingly was called "A City on a Hill."

A MISSIONS DEPARTMENT

Often, attractional churches will establish a missions department as a way to legitimize its missionary efforts and to show that it is involved in spreading the gospel to the ends of the earth. A missions department enforces a culture where a mission program is only a small piece of the church's overall vision. A missions program becomes just another program or department of the church that mainly serves to support "real" missionaries both locally and globally. This culture does not seek to promote the notion that all believers should be missionaries in their own communities. Instead, the missions function is relegated to others, and the church is not directly involved. Its role is to support "real" missionaries or an organization that is involved directly in ministering to the needs of the poor, orphaned, and widowed. The church should be supporting missionaries and agencies, but it should not excuse itself from being sent and joining in God's mission. Attractional churches incorporate a missions department as another program on the menu, mainly tasked to show and support what others are doing in their missionary efforts. In a post-congregational era, the church needs to see itself as missionary and being on mission should be at the center of everything it does. This is especially true since society at large is not being drawn to the lure of the attractional church like in times past.

REDEFINING SACRED SPACE

Some of this pressure can be alleviated if church plants can redefine sacred space. Gatherings in informal and cost-effective settings can alleviate the financial burden of the church. Also, faith communities should start thinking in terms of "movements" and "clusters" rather than something that is static and established. In his book, *Church Morph*, Eddie Gibbs develops the "cluster model," designed around "the core belief that God intends people to live out their faith in communities of fellow believers within their own cultural context."[72] God's people are the temple of the Holy Spirit. What makes space sacred is the indwelling of God's Spirit in the gathered community of faith.

This vision of the church as the people of God with the indwelling of the Spirit places less preoccupation with the building. A missional community discards the misconception of needing to have a formally consecrated building to be viewed as legitimate. According to Peter Ward, the use of the word *ekklesia* in the New Testament, suggested a "more fluid or networked kind of community based on small groups."[73] In the Primitive Church, groups of believers met in clandestine gatherings, mainly in homes, unable to be openly visible fearing Roman persecution. Today, the same underground faith communities exist in some countries around the world that are closed to Christianity, like China. Regardless, the Church has been able to spread despite these challenges.

Leaders, who think in terms of movements, are not restricted or distracted by the trappings of what the church culture deems appropriate for a gathering place. The location and building are not at the center of the missional community and the structure is not the glue that holds it together. In the attractional model, congregations become so reliant on the building for worship and fellowship that, if the structure were taken away, the faith community would collapse. In an attractional church, relationships can often remain surface-level, not reaching beyond church life to the everyday life that exists away from church property.

Pursuing Efficiency

Thinking of more efficient and creative ways to gather has the potential to focus less on the finances and physical structure. Considering the vast changes in the post-church culture of America, fluid and naturally forming faith-communities present viable options. The mindset of guaranteeing successful churches by planting static and permanent worship sites will likely be harder to sustain in today's uncertain, flexible, and

---

72. Eddie Gibbs, *Church Morph*, 122.
73. Peter Ward, *Liquid Church* (Peabody, MA: Hendrickson Publishers, 2002), 10.

constantly changing environment. The era when it was customary for the majority of families in America to wake up on Sunday morning and go to an established worship site is fading.

As society transitions deeper into a post-church culture, the church will feel more like an outsider, even in the realms of society where it once was an insider. Seeing results shortly after applying a previously successful formula will likely not be the norm. Finding creative and efficient spaces for worship will be invaluable in an increasingly secular society. The church needs to move away from the mental model of bulky, centralized, and costly worship sites. Attractional churches will be more difficult to sustain as the church enters the new era filled with representatives from the younger, postmodern generation. Church plants should move away from static and permanent mental models to more fluid and loose ways of functioning. In the words of Peter Ward, "Networked, informal contact between individuals and groups will replace monolithic meetings and formalized friendship."[74] Efficient worship space will help sustain the church over the long haul considering the expenses incurred in attractional churches. Informal and organic relationships will be the glue that binds the church together instead of a building.

Sharing Sacred Space

Building projects and commercial spaces require enormous financial support. To keep up with the expenses that sustain a worship site, the emphasis will be on giving. Attractional churches rely heavily on dollars to keep the machine going. Church members are the ones who are sought out for their tithes and offerings to cover building projects, mortgage and rent payments, and other expenses related to building use. It has been my experience that, when the church gets into financial difficulties, the congregation will feel increased pressure from their leaders to give more. The decision to share worship spaces can greatly alleviate the financial burden of the congregation, especially when there are worship sites that have declined in attendance in recent years and have space available. As society

---

74. Peter Ward, *Liquid Church*, 47.

transitions into a post-church culture, the pattern of struggle and difficulty in planting building-heavy churches will most likely be the norm rather than the exception. The choice of sharing space with another congregation is an efficient option. Church plants should be diligent in finding creative ways to share space so as not to burden themselves with the heavy cost of having bulky, centralized, and established buildings.

The Podshare System

Podshare is a company that has revolutionized the use of living/work space in urban areas of California. Some millennials are trading in traditional housing arrangements for flexible, cost-effective, and communal living experiences. In the Podshare system, there is no security deposit, no moving of heavy furniture, no time-consuming trips to the grocery store. The Podshare system caters to a variety of clients. Residents may include travelers who need a place for a few days, similar to a hostel. It can also be used for "transitioners" who need temporary housing as they look for a more permanent living arrangement in an apartment or house. This temporary housing arrangement through the Podshare system is ideal for individuals moving into town for employment. Additionally, long-term residents, who are busy professionals or freelancers, often prefer greater flexibility. These residents do not want to commit to a mortgage or lease but prefer the versatility that the Podshare system offers.

In these living spaces, all of the beds are in one room, which stimulates conversation and relationship, solving the loneliness problem among many Americans. Additionally, all "podestrians" have access to the kitchen, which also has communal food where residents can share a meal together. Elvina Beck, CEO of Podshare, said the company is built on a "sharing economy."[75] Residents share tables, desktop computers, and printers when working on projects or assignments. They can even share bikes. This mode of transportation is the preferred method, especially in downtown areas where parking is limited and traffic is significant. The

---

75. Nicholas Slayton, "The Invasion of the Pod People," Los Angeles Downtown News, June 6, 2016, accessed September 7, 2016, http://www.ladowntownnews.com/news/invasion-of-the-pod-people/article_44368992-29d0-11e6-adfd-1724fb105cd2.html.

Podshare system is built for community and friendship where residents share spaces and learn to get along despite their differences. This system is efficient and creative and opens the possibility for other innovative ways to share space. The church should consider different models in order to rethink the use of sacred space in ways that promote community in a cost-effective manner.

Third Places

Attractional churches can burden congregants with the finances needed to operate an expensive, established location. For this reason, particularly in building use, missional leaders today need to find efficient ways to use space in third places, as John W. Kennedy proscribes in his article, "Subsequently, AG [Assembly of God] congregations today are convening in all sorts of settings that a generation ago seemed unimaginable, including warehouses, schools, movie theaters, converted barns, coffeehouses, houses, and even fitness centers. One-sixth of all U.S. AG congregations have started within the past seven years."[76] This is especially true in a post-congregational culture, where society-at-large is not predisposed to support the attractional church model. Church planting initiatives need to consider third places seriously since they can be more efficient and cost-effective. They are also environments in which the church can interact with nonbelievers, creating a greater likelihood to develop relationships with unchurched people. What is normally viewed as a worship center by church planters consists of seats in rows facing one direction toward an elevated pulpit and a stage for the worship team. These churches look like every other church in the neighborhood, many of which are in decline with members having difficulty sustaining their maintenance needs.

---

76. John W. Kennedy, "Redefining Sacred Space," *PE News* (May 26, 2015), accessed May 30, 2015, http://penews.org/Article/Redefining-Sacred-Space/#sthash.hO80OvHK.dpuf. In this article, the author's examples include one church starting in a gym and another in a business owner's coffee shop, which ideas are outside of the typical, traditional model.

Mistakenly, success by some church planters has been measured by their ability to acquire their own building with a sanctuary, parking lot, and space for program development. Having seats in rows facing a stage is a mental model that has been ingrained into the church culture of how the people of God ought to gather. Worshiping God in this manner has often been an automatic and uncritical way of practicing church, but which is difficult to sustain in a post-congregational era. Additionally, this mental model emphasizes the worship format more than fostering community. The template of lead pastor-over-elders-over-congregation attempting to attract outsiders has been the ingrained organizational structure for many church leaders and still predominates in American church culture. This is a one-size-fits-all pattern results in an extreme loss of creativity and innovation. Adopting one model has caused the church overall to "become stuck in the prison of tradition, architecture, or organizational structure that once had meaning, but which remain empty vessels."[77] The lack of creativity produces cookie-cutter styles of worship, except for arranging the furniture, painting the walls, and replacing outdated fixtures on occasion.

The resources required to operate a typical centralized and permanent worship center tends to place a heavy burden on the congregation. Building-centered churches become a heavy load to carry, demanding vast resources from the worshipers. In a post-Christian culture, these facilities become increasingly difficult to sustain as society becomes more unchurched. These facilities also tend to create a self-centered posture, having to resort to attractive and expensive methods for luring outsiders into the central building site. Yet enticing outsiders to attend services is the primary growth strategy since filling the pews provides the finances required for the church to stay afloat. Christian leaders should find creative ways for the church to gather that are more mobile and economically proficient so as not to overly burden the people. This will allow church leaders to serve more genuinely since they do not have to focus on the finances as much.

---

77. Koeshall, "Ecclesiology-To-Go," 15.

Downtown Ministry

In the downtown areas of larger cities, where real estate has skyrocketed and is becoming unaffordable, congregations are being forced to think outside the traditional "box." Stepping out of the typical paradigm in the inner city is especially important considering the costs associated with renting and purchasing real estate. What makes a space sacred is the Holy Spirit living in the hearts and minds of the believing community. Whatever space the church inhabits is not a priority when disciple-making remains central to the mission of the church. A tall, pointed steeple, protruding into the sky, calling all worshippers in the area to worship, is no longer a viable strategy to make disciples in the postmodern era where the authority of the church and its leaders has dwindled. The saying, "Build it and they will come," is no longer a philosophy that church leaders can depend on for growth.

One group in the downtown Houston area meets at the YMCA on Sunday mornings. Another group of medical residents meets once a month at someone's house or apartment since this phase of their career training demands so much of their time. This group simply would not be able to be a part of a traditional church because of their demanding schedules. Meeting on occasion with others going through the same challenges and trials, however, provides much-needed support and encouragement during this phase of their lives. While members of attractional churches may not identify with or understand their situation, for them there is no better fellowship than being with others who understand their unique challenges. Finding efficient and creative ways to worship and find fellowship with others is particularly important in today's fast-paced, technological, and diverse world. In a post-congregational society, thinking beyond the traditional models of worship will be of upmost importance.

The Townhome Transition

I worked for a mission organization that had a goal of planting new churches and developing grassroots leaders to start new ministries. I started working for this organization in the middle of a major organizational restructuring. One of the biggest changes they were experiencing was moving offices. Prior to the move, they were using a large church campus they had purchased from a dying congregation. This large building, complete with a gym, sanctuary, classrooms, and offices provided a whole lot of dead space. Additionally, the maintenance to operate out of this building was costing the organization thousands of additional dollars, which were given by faithful donors. It was not the most efficient use of space, and it was an older building that required a constant flow of handymen coming in to repair all sorts of problems. The building itself was a leaky faucet of sorts, continually draining their bank account.

The organization ended up moving into a four-story townhouse close to downtown Houston. The staff had their own work spaces, a room was outfitted as a conference room, and the copy machine fit nicely in the place where the washer and dryer had been. The second floor became a large living room with nice couches, rugs, and comfortable chairs, all of which made it feel like a normal home instead of an office. The staff completed all the same functions they had done in their old building except with drastically decreased expenses. The organization hosted meetings and gatherings on a consistent basis, inviting donors, church planters, and ministers to various events throughout the year. This townhome provided a homey feeling for all those invited. On one occasion, a guest had a hard time finding the townhome, thinking that the church next door was where the gathering was taking place. His difficulty came from not being able to visualize sacred space outside the regular confines of an established church building. He waited in his car for a while wondering if he had misread the time until he recognized someone familiar going into the townhome, and only then did he realize he was in the right place. He knew the organization had moved, but he never imagined that they would have moved into a townhome. It did not fit his mental model regarding the use of sacred space.

THE COKE BOTTLE ILLUSTRATION

Coca-Cola has been bottled in a variety of creative ways over the years as they have adapted to the changing climate with the objective of yielding maximum production and sales. The product has been packaged in different shapes, sizes, and quantities, but the taste continues to be delicious.

It has been sold in a 12-ounce bottle or can, 2- and 3-liter receptacles, and numerous other experimental packages. They have become experts in understanding the culture of the markets they are seeking to penetrate in order to gain market share. Coca-Cola has understood the need to identify with and understand the worldview of people groups worldwide. Today, 112 years after its invention, "94% of the people in the world recognize the Coca-Cola logo and product."[78] During the World Cup one year, I bought a Coke that came in a plastic container in the shape of a soccer ball. I told myself that I would keep it as a souvenir and not drink it, but could not resist so ended up drinking it despite my initial desire. Recently, I saw a miniature version of the normal 12-ounce can designed for more health-conscious customers who wanted to drink the product in moderation.

Even though the contents inside the containers remains the same, the packaging and marketing strategies change. As the church transitions into a post-church culture, the message of the Good News does not change, but the packaging could be more fluid depending on what is the best fit in any given context. The form that dominates today has been stuck in the same centuries-old pattern, typically a building with seats in rows facing the stage with a podium. Instead of planting another identical model from a sponsoring church in another part of town, the form of communal life could be shaped by the rhythms and patterns of the host community. This allows the Holy Spirit to work creatively, shaping the culture that is already there, instead of imposing one's presuppositions of what the church should look like.

The dominant attractional model is an overused and outdated package for reaching a postmodern population that does not seek out the traditional church to find meaning and to fill their spiritual needs. Yet this tired model is still heavily ingrained in America's church culture, which makes it difficult to see beyond it. Centuries after its invention, church planters are still following this inorganic blueprint of what other successful churches have done in the past. Instead of allowing the context to shape and mold the church, leaders apply artificial methods that seem more like an "add water and stir" recipe. Missional leaders should transition toward

---

78. Michael Sills, *The Missionary Call* (Chicago: Moody Publishers, 2008), 291, Kindle.

nurturing naturally forming communities that are shaped by the rhythm and flow of the host community.

A Listening Spirit

A naturally forming faith community requires a listening spirit that places the culture of the community first. This requires leaders to live in and among the host community. To develop solidarity with a host community, to listen and engage the people, and to better discern what the Spirit is saying and doing, a missional leader needs to become a resident of that community. Frost and Hirsch argue that the church is tasked with "contextualizing," which is "concerned with presenting Christianity in such a way that it meets peoples' deepest needs and penetrates their worldviews, thus allowing them to follow Christ and remain in their own cultures."[79] This requires a servant posture that sets aside all preconceived notions, ambitions, and agendas. When allowing the host community to dictate the shape of the church, the best leaders will emerge indigenously from the host community. These are individuals who understand the community, are invested in it, have significant influence among the people, and have established credibility and trust by the examples they have set. Winning the confidence of the host culture is not a quick and easy process. Indigenous leaders drastically facilitate the process of becoming a resident of a community, especially for those coming in from the outside.

Indigenous Leadership

Naturally forming faith communities do not seek to enlist already "strong Christians" recruited from other churches. There is less reliance on "already ready" ministry leaders. Instead, leaders are taken from the community in which one is planting. Leaders sprout out of the soil and emerge naturally. Developing indigenous leaders would prevent extracting other leaders from their communities. Indigenous leaders have the advantage of using their local influence to reach their own neighborhood. Focusing on connecting with persons of peace from within the community and

---

79. Frost and Hirsch, *The Shaping of Things to Come*, 83.

developing them to be leaders will better provide an insider's view of the needs and challenges inside the neighborhood which the church is attempting to reach.

Also, indigenous leaders play a significant role in the decision-making processes. Oftentimes, indigenous leaders carry less baggage and may be able to see beyond the typical attractional church paradigm. Their view is unhindered and clear from any preconceived notions of what a gathering should look like. Planting teams should avoid seeing themselves as "experts" and approach the neighborhoods they seek to reach with humble and teachable postures, seeking to learn from the host community rather than impose an agenda. Church planters should avoid taking the role of the "sage on stage," but instead become the "guide on the side" seeking to develop others through coaching and mentorship.

Oftentimes, leadership in an organic, naturally forming community is cultivated internally. A participant who stands out and shows leadership potential may be asked to take on greater responsibility, possibly initiating another group. Leadership is developed internally as abilities surface within the community. Transitioning these leaders into specific roles can be smoother since they have already been integrated into the community and have gained the respect of others. Missional leaders could naturally reproduce from within faith communities rather than being appointed in an established, centralized location. These missional communities can also partner with traditional churches, offering support to them, with the objective of reaching the community for Christ. To better understand the flow of a missional community, the example of a fitness station captures its rhythms and patterns of being.

THE FITNESS STATION CONCEPT

The fitness station craze that is supplanting the traditional gym helps conceptualize the differences between the attractional church and a missional community.

The number of these specialty gyms or fitness stations grew by more than 400 percent in the U.S. from 2010 to 2014, but traditional gym memberships were up by just one percent in the same time frame.[80] Sara Angle writes, "Harvard Divinity School researchers posit that group classes such as CrossFit and SoulCycle are filling a spiritual void at a time when organized religion is declining; that like religious organizations, group fitness fosters community and personal transformation."[81]

Sprinkled across American urban centers are clusters of busy, working people who have joined these fitness communities to accomplish their fitness and health goals. They are becoming more than a workout place in that they are also filling a spiritual void and giving many younger Americans a community of which to be part. Those affiliated with these groups develop meaningful relationships with others who are seeking to accomplish similar objectives. They support and encourage one another as they pursue their goals. The founder of 305 Fitness, with studios in Boston, New York City, and Washington D.C., says, "Community is everything."[82]

The Traditional Gym

Traditionally, a person who seeks to workout would normally join a gym and fill out the corresponding paperwork to become a member. Gyms like 24 Hour-Fitness, Gold's Gym, and Planet Fitness build enormous and costly facilities complete with weights, nautilus machines, racquetball courts, pools, fitness rooms, massage tables, and so on. This fitness model is a centralized, static posture that has lost significant market share to the more fluid and mobile fitness stations. In a traditional gym, it is not out of the ordinary to go for a workout and not talk to a single person the whole time one is there. Working out with the machines or weights tends to be an individual endeavor with little interpersonal interaction. Even in group exercise classes, participants rarely get to interact with one another. They finish their sessions and everybody swiftly leaves the space and carries on with their lives.

---

80. Sara Angle, "Get Fit," *Shape* (June 2016): 58.
81. Ibid.
82. Angle, "Get Fit," 58.

Building Relationships

In contrast, building community is in the DNA of the fitness stations. What keeps people motivated and affiliated with these groups is that they create instant camaraderie. A team approach is fostered where participants share the same goals and aspirations. In these clusters, relationships are nurtured, they know each other's names, and participants look forward to seeing one another. Many have friendships nurtured that also extend outside of the group where they become involved in each other's lives on a more personal level. Fitness stations become much more than just a place to work out and enhance one's physical well-being. They feel more like a family, where below-the-surface relationships are fostered and participants become involved in each other's development.

Journeying Together

When a participant was asked about her CrossFit experience she replied, "You'll often exercise with the same people, many of whom may become your friends and encourage you to work harder throughout the class."[83] Traditional gyms tend to foster individualism, compared to fitness studios where participants are involved in the growth of others who are learning essential leadership qualities. If someone misses class or focus, participants will notice and reach out to the person making sure everything is okay, which adds a layer of accountability to stay on course. In the words of Eddie Gibbs, these clusters provide "low hierarchal control with high peer accountability."[84] This fitness community becomes a family to its members and offers a solution to the loneliness many are feeling in America today. These kinds of groups are becoming church to many young Americans. The fitness station concept has many characteristics which could be replicated in the church order to foster community.

---

83. Angle, "Get Fit," 58.
84. Gibbs, *Church Morph*, 122.

Fluid and Loose

Fitness stations are flexible and can incorporate a variety of exercise routines into their plans because they are less reliant on established locations. To change things up, the group may decide to meet at the park, rock wall, track, or stadium. Participants can work out creatively because they are not limited to a central place like the traditional gym. A cluster may decide to train for the upcoming marathon and will tailor a training regimen specifically for those who want to run in it.

As seasons change during the year, the group has the liberty to adapt to these changes. This concept is much more fluid and loose than the rigid, static gym model.

The groups do not want to limit their exercise routines. For example, in the fall and spring, groups prefer to be outside, especially on beautiful days. Most participants have spent all day indoors at work so spending some time outside is literally a breath of fresh air. In the permanent and established gym, this freedom would not be as feasible. Just because a cluster is decentralized does not mean it is disorganized. An array of communities is formed by people with similar interests beyond fitness. The fitness station model is one of many different types of affinity groups. Communities of faith coming together around a shared interest can result in increased participation and connection. These interest groups can also provide an opportunity for believers to be incarnational among the unchurched, which is naturally conducive to building a bridge and sharing the good news of Christ.

Collaboration and Cooperation

The communication that occurs in these decentralized communities extends beyond the stations, and these groups could easily exist without a building if needed. There is constant back-and-forth communication among the group members as planning happens. The leaders coordinate with participants so that everyone can be on the same page. These decentralized groups are much smaller and, therefore, easier to sustain, avoiding the heavy overhead of traditional gyms. The groups are more intimate enabling participants to establish meaningful friendships. Although groups are smaller, participants tend to be better connected to one another. The pressure to increase the size of the group is never a factor because it would only take away from the camaraderie that is experienced with a smaller group. If the group gets too big and difficult to sustain, there is always the option of splitting it into two or more groups and having occasional combined gatherings. Groups can also relate, communicate, and connect with other clusters in the vicinity forming a network with shared vision and values.

Neighborhood Impact

Imagine the Kingdom impact that could happen in a community, much like a fitness station, that is intentionally seeking to follow Christ together. Personal transformation would eventually lead to community transformation through the work of the Spirit. The change in people's lives would extend outwardly to their communities, extending the Kingdom into the hardest-to-reach-places in the city. With a shared vision, these communities could be salt and light, bringing God's Kingdom to their neighborhoods through their examples as living witnesses of the gospel. The edges of this community are not rigid but open, making it accessible to people living in the neighborhood. These decentralized groupings can provide additional entry points for the unchurched to join a less-threatening faith community. The connection that is established by serving together toward a shared objective is powerful. When there is a shared objective, participants will feel they are a part of a team and contributing members. The Spirit works within the group creating fellowship and mission.

Staying Close

Creating community is much more feasible when individuals do not have to drive long distances for gathering. The notion of commuting to have community is difficult to sustain and nourish over time. Especially in many urban areas, relationships have difficulty developing below the surface when participants are having to commute. Building community close to where one spends the bulk of life is much more feasible and alleviates the burden of members having to fight traffic after work along with meeting the demands of life. I heard someone say, "You cannot commute to your mission field." Fostering community in one's own vicinity allows faith to become a natural rhythm of life instead of a pre-fabricated event on a certain day of the week.

Community Ambassadors

A missional community does not require the vast expense of an attractional church. Instead, following Jesus is the common ground that binds them together rather than a building. Participants encourage one another to stay on the narrow road and to represent him well as his ambassadors. This community of believers journeys together while seeking to live faithfully to Christ and embodying the Kingdom in their vicinity. There would be no pre-fabricated model for worship; instead, this community would take on a life of its own, shaped by the natural flow of life and the leading of the Spirit. Missionaries Anita and John Koeshall explain that the church's effectiveness depends on her "ability to follow the leading of the Holy Spirit's creativity, to understand the culture in which it finds herself, and to carry the Spirit into the context in the earthen vessel that is the community."[85] Even if a hurricane passed through and blew away their physical building, this community would still thrive because the bond they share is much deeper than just a location for fellowship and worship.

Closing Thoughts

The church is the body of believers. Two or three gathered in the name of Jesus (Mt. 18:20) are considered the church regardless of where they decide to meet for worship, whether it is the breakroom at work, someone's basement, a sports venue, a movie theater, or the backroom of a restaurant. There are no one-size-fits-all forms of community. It is not uncommon for someone to be a part a traditional church setting and, at the same time, be part of an informal gathering closer to home. One type of gathering should not be considered more legitimate than the other. One group of preschool mothers gather in an informal setting in a neighborhood for

---

85. Koeshall, "Ecclesiology-To-Go," 13.

support, contact, and friendship. Though largely comprised of Christian mothers, the group has welcomed others not affiliated with any church. This has been a way for mothers to connect spiritually and to reach other mothers in the neighborhood with the gospel.

The gospel spreads through the relationships that are built when believers choose to live out their faith as integral to their day-to-day lives. Through the connections that Christians make in their neighborhoods and workplaces, they can share their testimonies. Through ordinary believers living ordinary lives in the places where they spend most of their time, they can be salt and light and testify of their Savior. Missional author Michael Frost makes a powerful point by saying:

> My point is that we need to just let churches be what God directs them to be in their given setting. There is no one-size-fits-all blueprint for what a church meeting should look like. We can become obsessed with this discussion, constantly seeking what shape our public meetings should take to attract more attendees and ultimately more followers. What if we spent more time obsessing about how to change the world, our city, or our neighborhood?[86]

The church is the people with whom the Holy Spirit dwells. The church is not a location, and believers do not go to church. The temple of the Holy Spirit is the people of God who put their faith in trust in Jesus and recognize him as Lord. Trying to force a certain model and attempting to control how the church gathers will only limit the creative work of the Spirit. The church is not a building; rather, it is the people of God who, empowered by the Spirit, take God's presence into the world. Instead of using prefabricated methods and strategies of evangelism, members of the church body share their life and faith with others as a natural expression of their love for God and neighbor. Spread throughout the city, the church is comprised of non-ordained and non-professional ministers who integrate faith into every sphere of life. They insert themselves into their

---

86. Frost, *The Road to Missional*, 103.

neighborhoods and workplaces, identifying with the life struggles and needs of their communities spontaneously and naturally. Clergy persons have valuable theological knowledge that they can impart to educate and train non-professionals in order to promote sound teachings of the faith. But, clergy persons are not the center of religious life; rather they are members of the body, who are essential to edifying the church.

BIBLICAL INSIGHTS

In the Old Testament, the sacred space for worship was centered around the Temple. Worship was organized, methodical, and established. There was little flexibility and mobility since the Temple was the space where God's presence dwelt. When the Babylonians destroyed the Temple and forced Israel into exile, they had no choice but to learn to redefine the meaning of sacred space for worship while living in a hostile territory. They could no longer use the same models of worship that they had when they were in a privileged status. According to Beach, the displaced church needed to "find new ways of practicing their customs and religious faith in a climate that was often less accommodating of what the local population would have determined to be strange practices."[87] Today, as the church is pushed to the margins, it will be important to be efficient, creative, and innovative when it comes to defining sacred space.

The center of Israel's religious life was the Temple, and, once it was destroyed, the people were left dazed and confused because that location had given their worship structure, significance, and identity. The Jerusalem Temple was the location where Israel believed God's presence was particularly immediate. Beach writes, "The temple was the center of religious ritual and a reminder that Yahweh was reigning with and over his covenant people."[88] Their exiled state forced them to adapt and develop a new way to maintain communion with Yahweh without depending on the Temple. Their theological presuppositions were shaken and they had to radically alter their views to encompass a new paradigm shift. According

---

87. Beach, *The Church in Exile*, 711, Kindle.
88. Ibid., 672, Kindle.

to Beach, Israel would have to shift their view of Yahweh's presence, which had been restricted to the Temple, to being "present wherever he chooses to reveal it, including Babylon."[89] Beach adds, "God is depicted on wheels and mobile as his glory departs the temple and flees the land."[90] They would now be forced to rekindle their lost consciousness of being sojourners as they recalled their wilderness journey for forty years. It was through this testing period that Israel's dependency on the Temple would be shattered as they learned to be in relationship with God, who no longer was confined to a place built with human hands.

The following paragraph describes the worship community of believers in the New Testament:

> The church of Jesus Christ does not worship at a temple but has *become* the temple. God now lives both among and within his people, not in buildings but in a living community (1 Cor. 3:16-17; 2 Cor. 6:16-18; Eph. 2:20-21). This metaphor is implicit in the frequent references to building (e.g., Mt. 16:18; 1 Cor. 3:9; 2 Cor. 10:8; 13:10; Jude 20). Given that the church is the place where God dwells in his Spirit, people must live in unity with each other and in holiness of life. Integral to the temple was the priesthood. Under the new covenant, all believers have become priests (1 Pet. 2:9; Rev. 1:6; 5:10; 20:6), once more bringing into actuality the unfulfilled design of the old covenant (Ex. 19:6).[91]

After being baptized by John, Jesus received the Holy Spirit and began a "movement" by calling his disciples to follow him. He preached and taught about the Kingdom of God, the power of which was demonstrated as he healed all kinds of sickness. The concept of the Kingdom was central to his ministry and he saw himself as initiating God's reign on earth. Jesus told his disciples in Lk. 17:21, "the kingdom is within you," meaning that

---

89. Ibid., 758, Kindle.
90. Ibid., 754, Kindle. See Ezek. 1:1-21 for God no longer being restricted to Jerusalem.
91. Ryken, Wilhoit, and Longman III, eds., *Dictionary of Biblical Imagery*, s.v. "Church," 148.

they had access to the same restorative powers that he had. Jesus called on his disciples to follow him, which was the beginning of the Kingdom community that eventually would continue his mission, even after his crucifixion. Jesus appeared to his disciples after his resurrection, commissioning them to proclaim the gospel to all nations. Jesus ushered in the Kingdom of God and his community of followers would participate in its expansion. "With the resurrection of Jesus, the Jesus movement became the church of Jesus Christ."[92] The church was not a place but had become the people of God embodying Jesus's words, "For where two or three are gathered together in my name, I am there in the midst of them" (Mt. 18:20).

WORDS AND PHRASES TO REMEMBER

Mental Models: These are deeply embedded, automatic ways of functioning that do not make sense, primarily since the environment has changed and requires a different way of thinking and being.

Pastor-Elder-Congregation Model: The ingrained organizational structure in many churches today, lacking creativity and innovation, adopting a singular model of church. A cookie-cutter concept, where one-size-fits-all, usually rows of seats facing toward a stage with a pulpit.

Movement: A community of faith that is not static or fortress-like but seeks to remain loose and fluid. The New Testament church operated more like a movement, allowing it to stay allusive and mobile during a difficult time for Christians who were on the margins of society.

KEY VERSES TO REFLECT

Acts 2:42-47
Lk. 17:21
Mt. 18:20

---

92. Ibid.

DISCOVERY QUESTIONS

1. Identify and describe a mental model that may have developed in your life.

2. Describe a creative community that could be initiated in your neighborhood or workplace that does not fit the typical paradigm.

3. What was your favorite part of this chapter and why?

TRANSITION THREE

From Clergy-Led to Laity-Led Ministry

THE THIRD TRANSITION INVOLVES HELPING ordinary church believers comprehend their part in God's redemptive plan in a post-church era. Shifting from clergy-led to laity-led ministry places ordinary believers in the driver's seat of the purposes and plans of God in their lives.

CHAPTER 5

Bridging Ministry Roles

THE PROFESSIONAL MINISTER MOVEMENT

CALLAHAN COMMENTS ABOUT THE PROFESSIONAL minister movement that arose after WWII: "Whole denominations became preoccupied with the professionalization of ministry. Seminaries turned their attention to preparing and graduating, in the best sense of the term, 'professional ministers.'"[93] Denominations kept up with the same educational and degree prerequisites that other professions required of their employees. The training and credentialing process that professional ministers underwent created a huge disparity in preparation between denominational pastors and the laity they served, thus creating a separation between the ordinary believer and the ordained. This led to some full-time pastors feeling the need to justify the costs associated with their salary and benefits. For this reason, many pastors take on the bulk of the pastoral duties within the church so congregants feel they are getting a good return on their investment.

The professional minister movement created a culture in which pastors performed most of the religious duties because they were the "professionals," and the laity were ill-equipped and ignorant to perform such sacred tasks. The nature of leadership became serving inside a consecrated building and being responsible for the care and administration of the church. This separation of roles further extended the divide between clergy and laity. The role of the professional minister had its glory days and was effective in a churched culture, but in an unchurched culture this model

---

93. Callahan, *Effective Church Leadership*, 5.

has ceased to be functional. America can now be considered a mission field; indeed, other countries send missionaries to the U.S. What is needed is not more professional ministers but a transition to missional pastors. The professional minister movement arose in a culture where the general population felt going to church was important—it was "the thing to do" on Sunday morning. Within this culture, there was a preoccupation with matters inside the church premises, and the professional minister movement arose to meet the demands of a churched culture. This is no longer feasible in a post-church culture where a growing segment of the population does not find any value in going to church and are finding spiritual nourishment with other associations. Yet, professional pastors continue to be groomed for ministering inside sacred buildings, going through extensive training in seminary, and undertaking a formal ordination process.

These pastors are additionally equipped to function as managers, supervisors, or CEOs, allocating resources and personnel to ensure that the church runs efficiently. The job description of a pastor today requires him or her to be managerial, as one "who conserves and holds, protects, and preserves the material welfare and economic well-being of the institution."[94] These types of pastors are "transactional" leaders who are focused on the smooth operations of the institution whose priority is in maintaining the order and stability of the church they lead. The preoccupation with office administration, budget, programs, increasing attendance, sermon preparation, and maintaining the well-being of the church causes the mission to be self-serving. For the church to be effective in outreach, however, members need to learn to engage and interact faithfully in other realms of society.

THE PASTOR-CENTERED CHURCH

A pastor-centered church, just like the name insinuates, places him or her at the center of religious life, where he or she is tasked with dispensing spiritual products and services to the worshipers who attend services. As officially sanctioned pastors, their role is "doing" ministry while the

---

94. Callahan, *Effective Church Leadership*, 40.

majority are passively "receiving" ministry. In the pastor-centered model, there is a clear distinction between the role of the pastor as the one who "serves" and the laity who are "served." Some pastors still use robes and special garments, which only compounds the distinction between clergy and laity.

Additionally, a center stage with a pulpit in the middle magnifies the centrality of the pastor. The laity becomes merely a group of bystanders with little attention given to their calling in the Kingdom of God. This creates a culture that hinders the laity from serving to their full potential. Often, they are viewed as ill-equipped and lacking formal theological training, causing them to be passive and tasked in supporting the pastor's vision. The pastor's primary role is to make sure the worship service is conducted accordingly and the spiritual needs of those attending are met. The hope is that attendees can feel a sense of connection with the divine during this brief period so they can go back to their regular secular lives. Once their spiritual tanks are depleted after a long week, they can get a "fill-up" during the next service. The clergy/laity divide fosters dependency. This dependency compounds the sacred and secular divide worshipers experience. Connection with the divine occurs during Sunday worship, but the rest of the week is secular and void of God's presence.

CONFINED TO THE BUILDING

When the location of the church becomes central to religious life, ministry training often becomes learning how to serve inside the church in some capacity. The idea of the Christian church still being central to American culture is a characteristic that gave rise to training that focused inside the church building. There continues to be an educational philosophy in some institutions in which "training remains firmly committed to the model of preparing a professional clergy for a set of tasks considered to be 'ministry.'"[95] Some of these tasks boil down to knowing how to run and maintain church programs and volunteers, organizing the bulletin for the following Sunday's service, and preparing a three-point sermon. When

---

95. Guder, ed., *Missional Church*, 195.

ministry training is confined to the church location, however, there is a perception that falsely believes that the "world is seeking out the church" and "the minister serves inside the church."[96] Regardless of evidence to the contrary, these two premises assume that the church will continue to exist indefinitely in its present form and will always hold a position of influence in mainstream society.

While teaching a missional class at a Bible institute, I discussed organic, naturally forming outreach in the neighborhood. I explained the importance of building trust with those around us to earn the right to share the gospel and develop communities of faith where we live or work. As one student listened intensely to my lecture, I could tell she wanted to say something. She finally raised her hand to ask, "But how are you going to pick up the offering if you're not at church?" It was obvious that this student's preconceived notions of church were confined to a sanctioned building, formally consecrated as a house of worship, and a place where worshippers would drop off their tithes and offerings when the plate was passed around. Even when congregations seek to be proactive in reaching their communities, often relationship-building is bypassed and evangelism is narrowed to inviting neighbors to church with the intention of converting them into faithful members. The hope is that once neighbors are convinced to attend services, it will lead to additional committed followers who participate faithfully in the services, programs, tithing, and all other activities which constitute being a "good member."

Pastor as the Focal Point

As its influence in society continues to decrease, the church will have limited impact if it continues to operate from outdated models that do not thrive in a post-church culture. These practices of worship focus on matters inside of a church building, where the pastor alone performs the bulk of the functions, which causes many of the people to be passive and serve as spectators. Churchgoers become the audience for pastor-centered services consisting of front-led activities usually on an elevated stage overseeing

---

96. Callahan, *Effective Church Leadership*, 10.

the congregation. Pastors perform these tasks almost to perfection, making them the experts in ministry on church grounds. This model can be one-directional where the professional ministers "do ministry" while the laity "receive ministry."

Pastors trained at ministering inside the church have become experts at their trade when it comes to the order of service, delivering a three-point sermon with illustrations, baby dedications, baptisms, and other religious tasks. The pastor has little relevance to outsiders except when there is a life event such as a wedding or funeral, at which time they are sought out for their specialized services. Once the special needs are met, pastors are placed back into their boxes until the next life event rolls around. When these pastors leave the security and comfort of church and pulpit, they become like fish-out-of-water when called to engage their own neighborhoods. In this limited view, ministry has been narrowed to the functions that occur on the premises of the church location. This concept creates a divide between sacred and secular space in a church leader's life. The same sacred and secular divide is transmitted to the members pastors are called to lead. Spiritual life becomes defined as occasions for which congregants gather at the church for a service.

ONE-DIRECTIONAL MINISTRY

In a *solus pastora* model, the lead pastor is at the center of spiritual leadership and handles most ministry tasks. Most ministry functions revolve around the pastor, placing him or her as the primary dispenser of religious goods and services. Historically, the overwhelming focus has been monologue preaching, which is one-directional and non-participatory. The professional minister is exclusively tasked with preaching while the members listen. In attractional churches, one of the main strategies of drawing people is emphasizing the pastor's homiletical and rhetorical abilities. In contrast, Murray asserts that "New Testament texts" show a more collaborative approach to ministry where "Christians learned together, alongside discussion and multi-voiced participation."[97] There is a

---

97. Murray, *Post-Christendom*, 127.

false belief that when pastors can perfect their sermons using various tools for delivery and preparation, it will compel outsiders to want to hear the message being preached. The pastor does little to engage and be visible in the community because most of his or her time is consumed with the all-important tasks of preparing for worship on Sunday morning.

Congregational Managers

Additionally, pastors who serve in attractional churches become consumed with the administrative and managerial tasks of overseeing the operation of an established worship site. When these tasks consume the bulk of the pastor's time, it is likely that he or she will rarely leave the office. Virtually all of these functions can be performed inside a climate-controlled office, making it difficult to leave the comfort of the church property. The pastor is caught in a spiritual bubble and gradually becomes disassociated with the outside world. Pastoral focus is centered on pleasing the members who become the stockholders of the church, expecting to get their money's worth for their investment. The same level of entertainment for which people pay in the secular world is expected from the church service. The pastor feels compelled to cater to the churched since they are the ones on whom he or she relies for a paycheck. Focusing outside of the building and reaching the community may cause churchgoers to feel that they are being neglected by their pastor. This may cause them to withhold their support because they think the pastor's role is to focus on their needs. Pastors become overwhelmed with serving the members and meeting all their demands, while the task of reaching the community is neglected by the pastor.

Disconnected with the Outside

The pastor's attention is absorbed with the internal functioning of the church and the demands that are required from those attending. The impact these pastors have on developing others and reaching their communities outside of the local fellowship is limited because their energies are absorbed by internal needs. Their ministries are concentrated mainly on the church grounds, and their preparation during the week culminates at the scheduled service. On occasion, pastors will visit someone in the hospital or conduct home visitation, but their primary role is confined to making sure the services run smoothly. When pastors are absorbed with the internal needs of running a church, someone else needs to be reaching the community and society at large. When the pastor's focus is consumed with the church's internal needs, seeing beyond these borders becomes difficult. This explains why equipping and empowering the laity is important to extend the reach of the church. Unfortunately, pastor-centered churches are a model that is still heavily ingrained in America's church subculture. Making the transition from being internally focused to externally focused require pastors with a missional vision who see the laity as the greatest resource to reach the community. A missional pastor sees the laity as missionaries to their communities and workplaces. The missional pastor's task is to equip and empower the laity to fulfill the calling of God on their lives and then to model that lifestyle.

It is difficult for pastors to develop connections with people other than the congregation because their schedule is already filled with responsibilities of managing and maintaining the church. There are administrative duties, programming, life events (weddings, burials, baptisms, baby dedication, etc.), conferences, meetings, and the list goes on. The Christian subculture that exists keeps the pastor inside of a spiritual bubble and disconnected from the unreached community. The pastor lives in his own confined world, tasked with religious duties primarily on church grounds, causing him or her to be far removed to the outside world. The focus on the needs inside the church causes the pastor to become irrelevant to the community at large. The same focus the pastor adopts is transmitted by clear example to the rest of the church, making the whole body ineffective. A culture is created where the pastor is the dispenser of religious goods and the congregation is the consumer. This disassociation with the community in which the church is located causes both the pastor and the church to be ineffective in addressing the issues in its vicinity.

CURRENT MINISTRY TRAINING

Unfortunately, the belief that Americans still place high priority on going to church is an element of Christendom that is no longer viable. This perspective is in stark contrast to an "exile mindset" in which the church is an unwelcomed outsider.[98] As mainline denominations continue to decline, it is no longer suitable for leaders to be trained in the way they once were, emphasizing ministry primarily inside a church building. The type of training that focuses on ministry inside the church will only further isolate Christian leaders and make them increasingly ineffective and limited in their reach and impact. In their world, service to the Lord becomes exclusive to the programs and activities of the church, and being on staff at a church is the pinnacle of Christian service. Any type of work outside of this framework is considered inferior or less spiritual to the tasks of a full-time, staff leader. Staff members are seen to be in a better position to impact others who are coming to worship and as possessing a higher level of spirituality than the laypeople. The downside is that staff members become consumed with the maintenance and management of the various programs and activities of the church. Their absorption with the church's internal affairs causes them to neglect the broader mission, particularly in their own communities. This helps to explain why the role of the layperson in ministry needs to be revived.

INSIDE THE CHURCH BUILDING

Bible institutes and seminaries still train leaders in traditional, front-led styles of leadership, serving the congregation from behind a pulpit. The expectation is that outsiders will flock to the church and leaders should be trained to minister to them when they walk in the doors. Courses in church administration, systematic theology, and homiletics equip future leaders for clergy-led churches. Advanced seminary training is used as a pre-qualifier for pastoral positions, regardless if students possess the

---

98. "Exile mindset" means the mental reframing a citizen goes through when they are forced to leave their own country and adapt to a new environment as outsiders.

competencies to serve in this capacity. As in most arenas, knowledge does not equate to effective spiritual leadership. Additionally, there is still an educational philosophy for training Christian leaders in some churches and seminaries that is one-dimensional. Rising leaders are trained for service in an attractional, program-centered church. Instead, a pro-active exile posture for ministry needs to be promoted to confront the complexities of an unchurched society.

Training that would give students the tools they need to engage their communities and workplaces in an incarnational manner are virtually non-existent in most seminaries and churches. A few formal courses that would expose aspiring missional leaders to an "outside-the-box" incarnational lens would be missional theology and leadership, world religions, apologetics, learning a second language, workplace ministry, anthropology, sociology, small group dynamics, mentorship, culture and languages, non-profit administration, and community-based training. These subjects emphasize an outward-focused, people-centered educational philosophy that equips students to serve others and to make disciples in the communities they inhabit. With an incarnational mentality of ministry, it is more likely that Christian leaders will not stand behind a pulpit and preach. Instead, it is more likely that they will be helping neighbors move, attend birthday parties and weddings, or even tutor.

Unfortunately, many go into ministry with the expectation and hope that they will be leading a congregation from a pulpit, in a paid position with benefits, and have a parking spot with their name in front of the church building. Even if these positions are still available, they are rare, and all of the "stars need to be lined up" perfectly for someone to get such an endangered role. In one instance, I applied for a senior pastor position and proudly made it all the way through the process until only three candidates remained. Unfortunately, after months of interviews and speaking invitations, I was not nominated. The whole process was grueling and to go through it and not be nominated at the end was disappointing. I asked one of the board members how many applicants they had and she told me there had been more than 70 prospects. For this reason, Christian leaders should be careful not to set their minds too rigidly on paid, full-time positions, because there are simply not enough of them out there to go around.

Trained for Attracting

For the few who are given the opportunity to serve in a full-time capacity with compensation and benefits, their main duty to the church is getting people to the service. Church leaders in attractional churches lead in an invitational, come-and-join-us posture. These leaders follow the same practices they have learned from their pastors in the past, and this is how the attractional trend continues to the next generation. Attractional churches rely on signs, billboards, diverse programming, events and conferences, fundraising events, and other activities that seek to pull outsiders into its religious bubble. Their methods parallel a consumeristic society where business owners attempt to catch the attention and draw passersby. The church spends large sums funding outreach initiatives inviting outsiders to events on the church premises. The goal is that the outreach investment will pay off eventually, when the church can add more people to their membership list. The expectation is that the new members reached will assimilate into the internal activities of the church and support its internal goals, which includes giving and volunteering.

Outreach that seeks to draw people into their location becomes more like dragging them in, especially in a growing unchurched culture. These attractional methods worked with a generation that were predisposed to attend and participate in church functions. Since I am in the church subculture, every week I get hundreds of invitations from churches and various ministries inviting me to attend one of their functions. The church uses savvy marketing strategies, expending vast amounts of time and energy on literature, emails, social media, and other technology in getting the word out to as many people as possible.

Some churches use catchy themes and slogans on church signs and websites seeking to lure outsiders to become insiders. Some of these slogans say: "A Place Especially for You," "We Are Saving You a Seat," and "Come and Make Us Your Church Home." Although these slogans are inviting, church leaders cannot solely rely on "attractional" methods as their main evangelistic strategy, especially in a post-Christian era. In an unchurched culture, Christian leaders cannot assume outsiders will find an in-house service a compelling proposition on a Sunday morning especially when it is their "funday." Also, because a famous evangelistic figure is placed on a flyer, the church cannot deduct that the general population will be interested or even recognize the personality.

There is still a misconception that church-going is a central part of the American culture like it was in times past. This misconception remains among church leaders, who believe that organizing an event is still the main, effective strategy for attracting outsiders. Typically, the ones who accept these invitations and attend these events are already embedded in the Christian subculture. These individuals have been in the Christian bubble long enough that attending worship services and events becomes a regular social practice; it becomes a form of recreation. It is typically the few rather than the many who minister and take an active role during these events, further widening the gap between those who minister and those who are ministered to. Attending worship services and events take up significant time in people's lives but often there is minimal growth since most attendees are on the receiving end of ministry rather than on the giving end.

With a central and established location for worship, church leaders insist that the congregation's evangelistic duty boils down to inviting outsiders to church so that they can experience a worship service and find fellowship with others. This mentality promotes an "extractional" effect on individuals; however, the end result will isolate them from their communities. The relationships that are developed are contingent on outsiders meeting churchgoers on their turf. Relationships are fostered only after outsiders have taken the first step and attended a worship service. The central meeting location of the church then becomes the glue that holds relationships together. So long as outsiders are willing to meet the church on its turf, they will be welcomed and embraced.

This stands in contrast to a "go to them" posture where the church initiates relationships within the community on their terms and turf. These relationships are not contingent on outsiders eventually becoming churchgoers; rather, they relinquish any agenda and genuinely seek relationships with others with a humble, servant posture. Jesus said, "I did not come to be served, but to serve and give my life as a ransom for many" (Mt. 20:28). He stepped down from his glory where he was seated at the right hand of the Father, humbled himself, becoming a mere human and a bondservant without self-seeking in his heart. But when there is an attractional model of ministry, outsiders are the ones doing what Christ did in stepping down from their turf to enter the doors of the church.

IN THE TRENCHES

Christian leaders need training that will allow them to adapt and adjust to the new challenges in a post-Christian society. Missionaries who are preparing to be sent overseas go through specialized training to better navigate the culture. The same training overseas missionaries receive should also be implemented at the church level here in America. In Houston, Texas, more than 93 different languages are spoken on any given day. The world has come to Houston, but churches and seminaries still seem to function as if little has changed, continuing to apply methods that worked when America was considered a Christian nation. To increase the reach of the church, members should be trained to function as missionaries in the places where they live and work. This kind of training focuses on ministry in the trenches of society where Christians may feel unwelcomed and uncomfortable. However, dwelling among the people the church is called to reach allows Christians the opportunity to live out faith within culture and away from the comfort and security of the church building and Christian subculture.

The Tentacles of the Church

The clergy should realize that by empowering the laity, the "tentacles" of the church will extend to spheres in the community that the clergy alone would never be able to reach. In attractional churches, pastors just do not have the physical ability to meet all of the demands of the church internally, much less to be involved in reaching the community alongside the congregation. Members are the ones who inhabit the marketplace, schools, neighborhoods, and other realms of society—which are all the places the clergy will never be able to influence. It is only through the congregants that the reach of the church can be multiplied. In the words of Darrow Miller, "We may spend 50-75 percent of our waking hours and 60-90 percent of the years of our lives working," and "Classes need to be established to prepare church members to disciple the marketplace sphere that they occupy during the season of their working life."[99]

This distinct separation between the clergy and laity is detrimental to the ministerial development of the congregants because it causes passivity and dependence when lay members view the clergy as the sole providers of religious goods and services. This environment of dependency does not provide an atmosphere of empowerment. Paul R. Stevens claims that, throughout most of church history, there have been two categories of people: "those who 'do' ministry and those to whom it is 'done.'"[100] He adds, "Lay people are the object not the subject of ministry."[101] When laypersons go back to normal life after attending a scheduled service, they are left powerless about how to apply their faith the rest of the week. For many, going to church is just another box to be checked off during the week. Churchgoers feel that their spiritual duties have been completed for the week. It becomes routine, week in and week out, but no growth in missional capacity is occurring. Being a Christian mainly means being committed to Sunday morning attendance. Unfortunately, this approach

---

99. Darrow L. Miller, *Life Work: A Biblical Theology for What We Do Every Day* (Seattle, WA: YWAM Publishing, 2009) 1704-1713, Kindle.
100. Stevens, *The Other Six Days*, 31, Kindle.
101. Ibid., 33, Kindle.

is building "marginal" believers instead of missionaries who are actively participating in God's redemptive plan for the world.

EQUIPPING THE LAITY

While teaching at a few Bible institutes in the Houston area, I observed that most of students were comprised of regular church members with a desire to serve in ministry leadership in some capacity. Most had regular jobs as carpenters, air conditioning technicians, customer service representatives, accountants, teachers, stay-at-home moms, and other ordinary jobs. They comprised the "ubiquitous laity," which describes individuals of Christian faith who are committed to their church and usually have membership status, but are not recognized as official ministers or pastors. I discovered that many laypersons felt they had peaked in their local congregations, so they enrolled at a Bible institute to further develop their biblical knowledge and leadership abilities. They had registered to attend a Bible institute with aspirations of taking their faith and commitment to the next level. Many felt the Lord was calling them to greater challenges, so they enrolled to prepare for what was ahead. During one semester, out of thirty students, not one self-identified as a full-time pastor. Unfortunately, their vision for ministry opportunities was limited to full-time pastoral positions, causing most to feel disqualified since not all will have this calling or the corresponding gifts to fill this role.

EQUIPPING AVERAGE JOE

By equipping laypersons to be local missionaries, the reach of the church would extend beyond the four walls into the hardest-to-reach secular pockets in society. Most of the members of local congregations are ordinary, working citizens, not ordained pastors or ministers. Even though they may not be "professional" ministers for their lack of formal seminary training or credentialing, they are the ones who can have the greatest influence on the unchurched in the public domain. The laity are the most untapped resource to reach an increasingly unchurched society. The public domain, which includes government buildings, schools, corporations, hospitals, and community centers, are the spheres in society that congregational pastors find hardest to reach. Most spend their time operating within the Christian subculture by preparing sermons, attending conferences, and associating with other believers. Additionally, their job descriptions cause their schedules to be filled with the daily maintenance and management tasks of running a congregation. Empowering "Average Joe" with a missional mindset will cause local churches to be revitalized as they send out their members as missionaries to the mission fields in their own backyards.

The Unaccommodating Society

Laity empowerment is especially needed today considering the current trend in America where the church is increasingly losing influence and prominence in society, particularly among the younger generation. Because of the decline of religion, most European nations are now considered to be well established in a post-Christendom society. There is a popularized version of the European phenomenon in America that some scholars use in their writing. Even though the situation in America is not as dire as what has happened in Europe, some scholars argue that it is moving in the same direction. This is evident in most public spheres in American culture, including schools, hospitals, and government offices. In a post-church America, the new, marginalized status of Christianity will require the church to leave its religious turf and engage an unaccommodating society incarnationally. Considering the alarming increase of young people walking away from the church and society's increased secularization, the need to empower the body of Christ is more important than ever.

Closing Thoughts

The overarching hope for this chapter is to convey the need that the reign of God will manifest, not only through professional, full-time ministers, but through the ordinary, unrefined members—the laity—living in the trenches of society. These overlooked missional leaders need to broaden their ministry horizons and dismantle the ingrained belief that only a few are called to "anointed" ministry. This mentality will keep ordinary Christians from living into their full potential and fulfilling the calling of God in their lives. Placing pastors on pedestals, without acknowledging the importance of the ordinary people living ordinary lives with many opportunities for mission within their communities, devalues the role of the laity in body of Christ. This narrow view creates a system where the other parts of the body are not as integral to God's overall mission in the world.

A hierarchy of spirituality has created dualistic thinking within the church, where the work in which individuals engage outside of the confines of the church is viewed as secular or less spiritual. In such a divided world, Miller explains that occupations in "accounting, carpentry, filmmaking, the arts, farming, and homemaking are secular activities and thus lower activities."[102] Due to this faulty mentality, he adds, "it is best to leave the secular arena and go to into the spiritual arena so we can be 'full-time Christian workers.'"[103] For the church to fully impact society, it is vital for the laity to see themselves as missionaries sent to the places they live and work. It is through their daily affairs that they will serve as witnesses and give glory to God through word and deed.

BIBLICAL INSIGHTS

Even though a caste system is no longer relevant, some denominational circles still differentiate the clergy and laity in some congregations, thus creating a separation between the ordinary believer and the ordained. This separation creates the idea that some individuals are more called than others, but any such divide between clergy and laity is unbiblical. Steven writes, "Laity, in its proper New Testament sense of *laos*, the people of God, is a term of great honor denoting the enormous privilege and mission of the whole people of God."[104] As well, he continues, "laity was

---

102. Miller, *Life Work*, 622, Kindle.
103. Ibid., 618, Kindle.
104. Stevens, *The Other Six Days*, 46-48, Kindle.

never used by an inspired apostle in Scripture to describe second-class, untrained, and unequipped Christians."[105]

From Ex. 19:6 and 1 Pet. 2:9, Beale pens the following regarding an inclusive call for all of God's people to join him in his ongoing mission to all nations:

> Israel collectively was to be to God "a kingdom of priests and a holy nation," going out to the nations and being mediators between God and the nations by bearing God's light of revelation. Instead of seeing the temple as a symbol of their task to expand God's presence to all nations, Israel wrongly viewed the temple to be symbolic of their election as God's only true people and that God's presence was to be restricted only to them as an ethnic nation.[106]

A distinction between the clergy and laity was never intended in the Bible; this construct was a man-made creation. Stevens further elaborates, "The word 'clergy' comes from the Greek word *kléros*, which means the 'appointed or endowed' ones,"[107] referring to all of God's people. In his words, the church should be "full of clergy in the true sense of the word—endowed, commissioned, and appointed by God to continue God's own service and mission in the world."[108] He adds that the church is not only the gathered *ecclesia*, but is to be "dispersed in the world, the *diaspora*, in marketplace, government, professional offices, schools and homes."[109]

In 1 Cor. 12:28, the Apostle Paul asserts that some individuals are endowed with the gifts of administration and/or leadership. Even so, it was never his intent to describe those with these gifts as more spiritual and the ones called to carry out the bulk of the tasks of the church. On

---

105. Ibid., 46, Kindle.
106. Gregory K. Beale, "Eden, the Temple, and the Church's Mission in the New Creation," *JETS* 48/1 (March 2005): 15, accessed April 2, 2015, *ATLA Religion Database with ATLASerials*, EBSCO*host*.
107. Stevens, *The Other Six Days*, 48, Kindle.
108. Ibid., 51, Kindle.
109. Ibid., 68, Kindle.

the contrary, he writes, "And He Himself gave some to be apostles, some prophets, some evangelists, and some pastors and teachers" (Eph. 4:11). The functions of the various members of the body are different but essential for the body to operate properly, as the various parts work interdependently for building up the church. Leaders help manage and direct, but they should not be viewed as sole heirs of ministry or possessing a "higher calling" than anyone else. One member of the body is not more useful than another. As Paul puts it in 1 Cor. 12:14, "For in fact the body is not one member but many."

WORDS AND PHRASES TO REMEMBER

Clergy-Laity Divide: A caste system within the local churches that separates Christians into two groups, the clergy and laity. The clergy are those called into ministry, while the ordinary and untrained believers, the laity, are tasked with supporting professional ministers in their churches.

The Traditional Pastoral Role: There is a clear distinction between the role of the pastor as the one who "ministers" and the laity as the recipients of ministry. In attractional churches, the task of the pastor is ministering to the churchgoers who walk through their doors during one of the scheduled service hours, while the majority stand passively and serve as spectators.

An Equipping Station: A model of leadership where the church becomes a sending agency as members become missionaries, leaving the religious turf and moving toward the turf of the world. With an outward thrust, ordinary believers are equipped to integrate their faith into the places where they spend most of their time, where they live and work.

SCRIPTURES TO REFLECT

1 Pet. 2:9-10
Eph. 4:11-12
Rom. 12:4-5

DISCOVERY QUESTIONS

1. How can outreaches to the community become more like "drag-ins"?

2. How would you describe pastor-centered churches?

3. How do you feel you could begin to break the clergy-laity divide in your life that is keeping you from your full missional potential?

CHAPTER 6

Ministry Beyond the Building

Help from the Unexpected

While completing the work on my final project when I was finishing advanced ministry studies, I encountered a technological challenge. I did not have training in statistics that would allow me to present the data I had collected. This task required a level of sophistication that was beyond my reach, using programs to which I had little exposure. Measuring the results of this project was an essential component, and I felt rather powerless. I was forced to pursue help from outside my immediate ministerial and academic circle. I had grown accustomed to reaching out to professors and pastors within my ministry network for support and guidance, but it was different this time. The help received for the more technical aspect of this project came from laymen outside of my typical ecclesial community. Their education and expertise came from working in the corporate world. They were not part of the clergy nor were they serving in full-time ministry. Working with these professionals showed how easy it is to be blind to the potential present in local congregations. If I could tap into their expertise on this one project, imagine what could be done in local congregations with a multitude of gifted laypersons from a variety of fields and careers.

I also realized that they were not only gifted in ways most pastors are not, but these individuals could influence people in areas to which the typical pastor would never have access. A pastor could never have the same access to the coworkers with whom these Christian professionals interacted daily. They had earned credibility in the workplace, which gave them an insider's ability to influence the unchurched. Initially, it was not intuitive to seek help for this project from individuals who worked outside of church or ministry settings. These individuals had no agenda, and they would receive no benefit by giving of their time and energy other than knowing they were helping me with a project that could hopefully have Kingdom impact. They were individuals who came along unexpectedly, and who gave of their valuable time and honest assessments without asking for anything in return. These are the folks that often fill the pews of the church who are tremendously gifted and serve as God's representatives in their contexts.

The expertise these individuals offered to me came from the daily tasks they carried out that were part of their job description. Pastoral leadership should realize the talent and resources they have in their own congregations from ordinary working folks. The possibilities are endless when they see members of their churches as vital components to the work of the Kingdom. Pastors should be more intentional in finding creative ways for congregants to exercise their gifts and talents. This kind of support will lead them to integrate sacred and secular compartments of life with intentionality. Pastors should avoid living in a spiritual bubble, instead, seeking to understand areas outside of their day-to-day tasks from the people who live out their faith in society. If pastors and ministers only spend time in their own areas of expertise and influence, it is easy to become irrelevant and disassociated with the members of their churches and the world at large. With a better understanding of the contexts in which members live and work, pastors can better equip the church to be on mission.

Because I was willing to look outside of my usual circle of advisors, I attained a completely different worldview from working Christians who were attempting to live out their faith in their workplaces. If pastors can place themselves in the shoes of their congregants whose existence is mostly beyond the church grounds, it will allow them to equip these men and women with the tools they need to be local missionaries. Instead of attempting to get congregants to support only the internal needs of the church, pastors should take the opposite approach and see how they can support their congregants to living purposeful lives in the world. This posture of curiosity and solidarity can help congregants close the gap between the sacred and secular compartments of their lives in order to help them live with greater integrity. Below are the individuals with whom I consulted who were living out their daily Christian lives in society away from the church. I tapped into their knowledge and expertise to complete the technical portion of the project. Without their practical knowledge, measuring the results of my project would have been much more difficult. Names have been changed to protect their privacy.

Susan Logan, M.D.

Dr. Susan Logan, a physician at the Texas Medical Center specializing in pediatrics and internal medicine, is the first person I consulted who helped formulate a viable survey at the beginning of the project. While attending Sanford School of Medicine at the University of South Dakota, she wrote a handbook called *Medical Student's Handbook for Electives in Global Health*. She had been involved in medical missions, particularly in Zimbabwe, and her research in global health came from her passion to bring relief to poverty-stricken areas around the globe. Part of her research as a medical student included formulating a survey to capture student involvement in and perception to global health education. She helped me format the survey I used for my project based on her prior experience. Her completed handbook was a resource for those students who desired to incorporate global health electives with their medical education. It helped students plan and prepare for all the details associated with overseas travel as a medical student.

Bill Hirst, Economist

An economist and statistician at Litigation Analytics, Inc., Bill Hirst conducts analyses regarding economic loss in cases involving personal injury and wrongful death, including an analysis of earnings, with the related topics of education and occupation, non-wage benefits, non-market services, personal maintenance expenditures, and household decisions. He holds a Bachelor of Business Administration and a Master of Science concentrating in Economics. Hirst provided valuable assistance by transforming the data I had collected during the project into useable statistics. The only regret was not having him involved in the measuring process earlier in the project. He could have added some valuable advice before the survey was administered instead of working with the data that was already available after it had been collected.

JESUS LAINEZ, FINANCIAL ANALYST

A financial analyst with TMI Hospitality, Jesus Lainez was responsible for developing a valuation model for potential acquisitions and the existing portfolio of hotels using a variety of methods. He also was a third-year law school student at the time. He used his expertise by helping to transfer my survey tabulations into Excel. As with Hirst, it would have helped to have Lainez involved earlier in the project. His contribution came later when the survey tabulations had already been completed.

If I had not been open to learning about the lives of these professionals, their talent and expertise might have remained buried and undiscovered. Pastors should avoid staying one-dimensional in order to see the possibilities that can be accomplished through their churches using the gifts and talents the members already possess. Each congregant is endowed with gifts and talents that can have significant Kingdom impact in their homes, workplaces, and communities. If the church could see the body of Christ as greater than the different programs that make up their local churches, including Christians in government, healthcare, education, business, and more, the footprint that could be left for the sake of the Kingdom would be much greater. Pastors, intentional about identifying, developing, and nurturing the gifts and talents that make up the local body, will then be able to foster a people development culture in which they begin with the gifts and talents represented in the church body and develop programs on this basis. This is in stark contrast to starting with programs and attempting to force individuals in the body to fill these roles. Based on people's gifts, the pastor serves as coach and resource to help others achieve their God-given purposes. The pastor places his or her focus on seeing others reach their full potential and on ensuring that their ministries are people-centered rather than pastor-centered.

BROADENING HORIZONS

In local congregations where only a few leaders conduct most of the ministry, the regular worshipers may be underdeveloped and incapable of serving effectively in their own contexts. Many have grown to rely heavily on the clergy, even for basic spiritual tasks like prayer, one-on-one evangelism, and morning devotions. Unlimited opportunities exists for the laity to serve and make an impact, particularly in the places where they live and work, but they need training that will better equip them to serve in the "trenches" of society. Capable leaders within congregations have the tools necessary to begin the journey toward becoming missional. Unfortunately, their full potential is not being realized due to debilitating mental models. The laity needs a vision of reaching people in the public domain—where they spend most of their time—making them resident experts working in fertile ground for God's mission. Service in the home, neighborhood, and workplace should not secondary to ministry inside the official church location. Local churches are consumed by their internal needs, causing the laity to become ineffective in reaching their own communities. The fields are ripe for the harvest, but the laborers are few. Members could become the laborers who will reap the harvest and be the salt and light in a dark world.

Equipping the laity will drastically expand the reach of the church. Church leadership, intentional about empowering and encouraging congregants, will help them live out Great Commission in the public domain. R. Paul Stevens holds that "theological education begins to change when a congregation redefines its primary arena of ministry as the daily life of its members rather than in-house service."[110] As the cultural authority of the church continues to weaken and its voice is increasingly marginalized, the need for missional training for the laity will continue to be in

---

110. R. Paul Stevens, *The Other Six Days: Vocation, Work, and Ministry in Biblical Perspective* (Grand Rapids: Eerdmans, 1999), 174, Kindle.

demand. This training will distribute the spiritual tasks of local churches more evenly, dispersing their various roles throughout the body. This will allow "Average Joes" to take a more active role in growing the Kingdom. Churches that serve as empowering centers will reset their focus on the sending of local missionaries into surrounding communities.

THINKING OUTSIDE THE BOX

Adam Melendez was a student who mentioned his desire to be a full-time pastor. His dilemma was that he was not sure how he could continue to run his business and be a pastor at the same time. He felt he would have to decide between being a pastor of a congregation or running an air conditioning business. After discussing these two facets of his life, he articulated that his business could support his ministry objectives and he could be a pastor to the employees he supervised. He had great influence over his employees in that he hired young men and trained them, allowing them to learn a trade. He discovered that the greatest impact he could have was with the very people he interacted with every day. Oftentimes, up-and-coming leaders can have a limited view of how they can develop their ministries since they are following the set patterns they have learned from those who went before them. Adam had developed a mental model that did not allow him to integrate his pastoral aspirations and his work life. With a new mind frame, he would grow his ministry and spread the Kingdom through the people he encountered in his business.

For some time, Adam had a compartmentalized view of ministry. Service to the Lord happened primarily on church grounds during one of the scheduled services, either Sunday or Wednesday night Bible study, while his work life was in the secular arena. This area of his life was not as spiritual as when he served at his church. At work, he felt he was not serving the Lord to the fullest capacity like he was when preaching a sermon. He greatly enjoyed the opportunities his pastor would give him to preach on Sundays. Standing in front of the congregation and delivering a well-thought-out message made him feel important and recognized. When I began to prompt him about seeing himself as a pastor not only on Sundays but throughout the week, this form of ministry was not as attractive to him. Daily working side-by-side with one's employees is much more demanding, because Christian leaders must set an example throughout the week and not just during church services. It is easier to be on one's best behavior for a few hours at church. For Adam to be a pastor to his employees, however, he would have to be Christ-like in the realm of life where he spent most of his time, where it would naturally be more difficult to remain faithful to the Lord's teachings.

Adam would be required to reflect the gifts of the Spirit (Gal. 5:22) during long days working "in the trenches" alongside his employees. On hot summer days, crawling into attics where air conditioning units are located can test the faith of the most spiritual. This requires greater commitment to following the example of Christ and should not be considered secondary to pastoral functions inside the church building. Adam can gain the respect and trust from his employees by reflecting the gospel in the example he gives to his employees. This is where his Christ-like character is truly put to the test. It would be perfectly reasonable for him to one day serve as a pastor of the church, but until then, he could be a pastor in an area of his life where he had influence on his employees, many of whom were unchurched. We concluded that he could serve in his church but also serve in his workplace. There was no need to separate these realms with one being more spiritual than the other. I was truly impressed when he came to my house to fix my a/c unit. He had a helper with him who had limited experience, and Adam was coaching him on running some tests. After they had finished their work, we had a moment to talk to this young man about spiritual matters and his faith in Christ. This conversation came about naturally, as part of the normal ebb and flow of life.

Full-time Ministry

Christian leaders who attend Bible institutes and seminaries take the step of seeking higher education hoping eventually to secure a full-time position and become a professional minister in some capacity. In times gone by, when the church was still heavily influential in society, pastors could look forward to a salary, professional expenses, and retirement benefits.

Some were even given a parsonage with all housing expenses paid. As the church moves to the margins, these opportunities are becoming less available as the local church diminishes in its former role as the center of religious life. When the standard curriculum trains leaders for congregational, professional ministry, this culture fosters the idea that the objective for receiving formal ministry training is eventually to become a full-time minister. This can no longer be the end goal, because, as Callahan states, "The day of the professional minister is over. The day of the missionary pastor has come."[111]

As I taught students preparing for ministry, I felt they had the wrong impression, which was that upon graduation they would transition to a full-time ministry position inside a local church. It was either that, or their pastors would have something lined up for them as a reward for their hard work of getting through the training. Over the years, I realized that even the schools' sponsoring denominations might not have positions available for them. The reality is that they are somewhat powerless in helping students find full-time ministerial work considering there are more churches closing than are opening their doors. This is partly due to the diminishing influence that mainline denominations have on contemporary culture and the decreasing numbers attending Sunday services. It is not my intent to be negative, but it is important that the next generation of leaders understand the changing society that is not as accommodating to Christianity as times past when the church held a central place in the life of Americans.

Expanding Ministry Horizons

No longer is it productive to promote a culture where service to the Lord is limited to involvement solely in the programs and activities of the local church, no matter how sincere and dedicated people may be. Leaders need to have their horizons broadened regarding the meaning of ministry so that they can begin to discover opportunities in some of the other compartments of their lives as fertile ground for God's mission. Often, their own congregation is not supportive to outside initiatives beyond the

---

111. Callahan, *Effective Church Leadership*, 3.

building because it may distract from the ministries within the four walls. Under these circumstances, Christian leaders may have to find a support system on their own to help in prayer, encouragement, and accountability as they seek to be faithful to the Lord's purposes for their lives. Service outside the church should not be considered less of a priority and secondary to ministry inside the official church location, especially when the church is rapidly becoming irrelevant to a major portion of society. The best scenario would be that church leadership empowers, supports, and trains congregants to make an impact in their neighborhoods and workplaces because it is part of the God's heart and mission regardless of specific benefits to the church.

Most churchgoers work regular jobs as carpenters, air conditioning technicians, customer service representatives, stay-at-home moms, and other ordinary jobs. Because of this reality, churches and seminaries could benefit by the incorporation of training that focuses, in Stevens's words, "not only the life of God's people gathered, the *ekklesia*, but the church dispersed in the world, the *diaspora*, in marketplace, government, professional offices, schools and home."[112] For the church to stay relevant and engaging, regular churchgoers need to see themselves as fellow missionaries instead of relegating that role exclusively to professional ministers or pastors. Service to the Lord can no longer be confined to volunteering in one of the internal programs and activities on church property. The whole people of God need to participate in God's mission as they engage the world as exiles in their communities, workplaces, and homes.

THE BODY HAS MANY MEMBERS

Callahan writes, "People lead in direct relation to the way they experience being led."[113] Clearly, it is no longer feasible in a post-Christendom culture for the end goal of training leaders in churches and seminaries to one day become full-time pastors or serve inside the church in some capacity. For too long, ministry has been taken as serving exclusively inside the local

---

112. Stevens, *The Other Six Days*, 65, Kindle.
113. Callahan, *Effective Church Leadership*, 20.

church when other areas outside of the local church are also important to God's mission. With the full support of their congregation, the laity in churches need to be trained to lead incarnational initiatives in the places where they live and work. Neighborhoods, workplaces, and homes are fertile ground for outreach and need to be integral to God's mission in the world. The Apostle Paul expressed the sentiment when he addressed the church in Corinth:

> And the eye cannot say to the hand, "I have no need of you"; nor again the head to the feet, "I have no need of you." No, much rather, those members of the body which seem to be weaker are necessary. And those members of the body which we think to be less honorable, on these we bestow greater honor; and our unpresentable parts have greater modesty, but our presentable parts have no need. (1 Cor. 12:21-24).

When ministry focuses inside the church, Christians are led to envision the verse above as confined to the individual members serving within local congregations. The parts of the body become members serving as Sunday school teachers, ushers, parking attendants, elders, and deacons. The pastor is the member who is responsible for the most visible position, leading from behind the pulpit. The pastor will encourage members to serve the Lord, which usually is narrowed down to volunteering in some capacity in one of the departments of church. The pastor may announce a new volunteer as someone who has decided to "serve the Lord" by leading the children's, men's, women's, or any other department. These programs can be fruitful in edifying the church, but they can also restrict ministry only to serving inside the church in some capacity. This mindset excludes the areas where most congregants spend the bulk of their lives—their neighborhoods, workplaces, and homes. Oftentimes, a "centrist" culture is promoted that elevates ministry inside the church and relegates other areas as secular and less spiritual.

Where ministry is centered around the pastor and the various departments of the local congregation, it inhibits the body to work to its full potential because the full array of talents and gifts are underrepresented. This narrow view of ministry creates a caste system where there are different levels of service. The tasks inside the local church are the most spiritual, and being a congregational pastor is at the pinnacle of all levels of service. The responsibilities that individuals have in the other compartments of life are rarely given any importance as integral to the mission of God. Yet, the body of Christ consists of members scattered throughout society in classrooms, companies, government offices, construction sites, and so on. Despite this, little attention is given to equipping the members of the body to function as local missionaries in the areas where they can have the most profound impact.

Ordinary Members

Churches should move away from a settled and established posture and move toward a more allusive ministry model where ordinary people living ordinary lives are equipped and sent out to their communities as missionaries. This model will be referred to as a *missional* church. Churches functioning as equipping stations will capitalize on the many opportunities the laity have for mission in their daily lives, which also places greater value on their role in body of Christ. The attractional model tends to compartmentalize the sacred and secular spheres, separating church as a place where religious products and services are administered by professional ministers. Work is conducted in the secular arena, and, understandably, the laity struggles to be effective in this sphere with the ministry to which the Lord has called. The Apostle Paul exhorts the church to give greater honor to the parts that seem to be weaker or are perceived as less essential (1 Cor. 12:22-23). Looking down on the professions of ordinary Christians can hinder the work of the Kingdom when only some parts of the body are considered useful or capable in advancing God's mission.

Diversity of Talents

The Apostle Paul compared the church to a body, indicating that the church was to be "a living organism, not a religious organization."[114] He also stressed "the dependence of members on one another."[115] This attitude considered the diversity of gifts and reinforced mutual responsiveness and reliance. He further described the church as comprised of members with a diversity of gifts for ministry, for "the equipping of the saints for the work of ministry, for the edifying of the body of Christ" (Eph. 4:12, NKJ). The word for "ministry" utilized in the Greek is *diakonos*, which also is translated to "service." Ministry is not confined to a special class of ordained pastors with full-time employment status or occurring only in the religious zone during the scheduled service hours. Rather, it is the act of serving others in the name of Christ in order to "build them up." This is a responsibility charged to all Christians.

An Equipping Station

Wise church leaders demonstrate intentionality in the empowering and equipping of their congregants to grow as local missionaries. Being intentional about equipping churchgoers to live out their faith by teaching them to integrate their talents with Kingdom purposes could greatly change the impact churches have in the world. Formal missionary training should not be reserved only for those preparing to go overseas as foreign missionaries. Instead, churches should provide the essential theological, cultural, and practical foundations to help their members respond confidently to their missional calling, starting in their spheres of greatest influence, their communities and workplaces. We are living in a time where our society is becoming increasingly secular and pluralistic. Churches are increasingly feeling like outsiders in society as if they were in foreign territory. The general population does not seek the church and its worship services as it once did.

---

114. Ryken, Wilhoit, and Longman III, eds., *Dictionary of Biblical Imagery*, s.v. "Church," 148.
115. . Ryken, Wilhoit, and Longman III, eds., *Dictionary of Biblical Imagery*, 148.

Preparing teachers, college students, customer service reps, and medical practitioners to implement incarnational initiatives in their communities, workplaces, and homes will broaden the reach of the church. With missional training, ordinary believers are better able to integrate their faith into the places where they spend most of their time—where they live and work. The church becomes a sending agency as members become missionaries, leaving the religious turf and moving toward the turf of the world. The church must relinquish its agendas that focus mainly on internal needs. A teacher spends at least 40 hours a week with students. A Sunday school teacher may spend between 2-3 hours with her students on a given Sunday. Yet, churches normally do not acknowledge service outside of the church as ministry. Just by the number of hours dedicated per week, it is obvious which teacher has the potential of having the greatest influence on students. In the same way that missionaries infiltrate Chinese culture by teaching in their schools, a similar strategy could be implemented in post-church America. The church needs to be fully supportive of such efforts and provide the necessary training and encouragement for working people in their congregations to live purposefully in the workplace.

Mission Outpost

Churches might consider functioning more like mission outposts. In the words of Callahan, "A mission outpost may have a tent, but it does not have a fort."[116] From a military perspective, an outpost is a place to which soldiers can retreat and refill their depleted ammo, get medical attention, nourish their bodies, and reassess strategies against the enemy. The members of an outpost spend most of their time away from the central location, so the objective of coming together after a long hard battle is not to stay but to recharge and restock, knowing they will be going again out shortly. The organizational structure of a mission outpost has as its main priorities: 1) Focus on matters outside of the station, where the battle is taking place; 2) Assign most of the recruits or volunteers to posts outside of the

---

116. Callahan, *Effective Church Leadership*, 28.

station; and 3) Dedicate the bulk of mission energy to strategies for the battlefield.

The same ideas of a mission outpost could be applied to the church for it to move toward becoming missional. It is a matter of priorities. As an example, if 90% of the organizational structure of a church focuses on internal matters, while 10% focuses on matters outside, then it is a highly attractional church. Vice versa, if 10% focuses on the internal matters, while 90% focuses on external matters, then it can be considered a missional church. There are churches that are highly attractional, but are slowly moving toward becoming missional, allotting more and more focus, time, and resources toward outward objectives. The energy of the missional church is directed outward because that is where the battles are won. It continuously prepares its troops to "go and not stay."

POLICE STATION

The best way to describe the church as an equipping station was illustrated in one of my classes by a student who, in her attempt to understand this idea, articulated openly what she was conceptualizing in her head. She compared the idea of the church as an equipping station to a police station. Before their shift, police officers arrive to their assigned stations to relieve fellow officers from previous shifts. They conduct a "hand off" so the officer who is coming in knows what to expect going into his or her shift. The outgoing officer passes down essential information from his or her shift that will help the incoming officer be successful. There is extensive communication and training that happens as officers discuss potential issues and lessons learned. Everyone at the station is involved and participating, taking and giving input.

The information that is being shared at the station is vital as the police officers move to their assigned posts. Even after they leave the station, there is ongoing communication between the officers through their radios. Even though they are dispersed throughout the city, communication does not end once they leave the station. There is an ongoing sharing of information as they patrol the streets using available technology. Completing the cycle, valuable information they receive during their shift is then communicated to incoming officers for the next shift. In a collaborative approach, officers share their thoughts on how certain situations could have been or needs to be handled. There is reciprocal sharing of information, support, and camaraderie as they "gather" then "scatter." Even though there is appointed leadership, the officers feel as if they are part of the team, working together toward achieving their shared mission.

Go and Not Stay

There is no limit to the impact local churches can have in the world when regular members live as the hands and feet of Jesus being sent out by their local churches as missionaries to their homes, neighborhoods, and workplaces. Yet, this is only possible when sending churches equip their people with the necessary training to succeed and be effective. Instead of attempting to retain people so they do not leave, the church can become an equipping station where members meet for encouragement and support so they can go back out into their communities with renewed vitality, to be salt and light in a difficult and hostile world. The church is, then, no longer as intensely concerned about retaining and assimilating churchgoers to their activities and programs. This only extracts them from the places they live and work and makes them ineffective in building relationships in the communities they inhabit. Churches that learn to loosen their grip on their congregants realize that their object is not to get them to "stay," but rather to make sure they have the tools and training they need to be effective missionaries in their neighborhoods.

Missions Misconceptions

Misconceptions abound regarding what missions is all about. For some, missions comprise an occasional event to support and raise funds for an overseas or other endeavor by an official missionary. For others, missionary work is exclusively an overseas enterprise and their purpose is to support those efforts financially and logistically. In this mindset, missionaries are "only those who left secular work to dedicate themselves to 'spiritual' work full-time,"[117] says Miller, usually in faraway places. Some churches have a missions department that focuses on bringing awareness to overseas missionary work to the exclusion of local missionaries living ordinary lives. Missionaries are predominantly those who have chosen to go to a distant land and who need the support of local churches for their continued work.

Another misconception of missions is when an "event" or "conference" becomes the focal point and the task of leaders is to "lure" and "attract" outsiders to "a certain place, in order to connect with God."[118] Once participants have been drawn together, they can be evangelized by using charismatic preachers, nationally known worship leaders, and cutting-edge stage lighting to stir up emotions and soften hearts. The goal is to get as many "decisions" as possible and the success of the event is measured by this number. This view of mission places an emphasis on "where the church meets, the style of service, or even the structure."[119] Additionally, great effort is made to bring attention to key figures, such as pastors, speakers, and worship leaders, who are charismatic and well-known in Christian circles. These figures are utilized as the main draw and their pictures are visible on advertisements. This strategy of evangelism seeks to compel "outsiders" to attend a service using robust marketing tactics often used by businesses to promote their products.

I want to stress that overseas and event missionary efforts have their place, and many have come to know the Lord through these efforts. My point is that the same amount of emphasis given to these activities must also be given to engaging local communities and workplaces in everyday life. The impact that ordinary folks could have in their contexts could be tremendous if they would see missions more holistically, as an "embodied way of life" instead of a "result-geared confrontation"[120] or an overseas endeavor. Through "demonstration" of the gospel, a mentality in which "you

---

117. Miller, *Life Work*, loc 991, Kindle.
118. Ibid.
119. Gibbs and Bolger, *Emerging Churches*, 96.
120. *Ibid.*, 80.

say the gospel by living it"[121] in everyday engagements and interactions, opportunities would open naturally to the sharing of the message of the Kingdom as people go about their business.

BI-VOCATIONAL MINISTRY

With Christianity's loss of the status from former times, bi-vocational ministry is becoming more of a realistic option in America. If students are set on full-time pastoral positions, a secular job can be a means of making an income until a position comes their way. The church cannot lose sight that these positons in the marketplace are also white for the harvest and needing more laborers to go and reap. Sometimes aspiring full-time pastors may have to wait it out a few years before something comes available. Until that time, they need to be sure they have a way to make a living. Christian leaders would do well to remain marketable to employers in the workplace outside of a ministry setting. There are instances when students spend significant amounts of money to prepare themselves for full-time ministry. Some even take out loans to fulfill educational requirements for ordained, institutionally sponsored pastorates. Unfortunately, some put all of their "eggs into one basket," and have no transferable skills to perform work outside of a full-time ministry context. All of their training and education is given toward ministry in a formal, full-time church setting. Students do not have careers to fall back on in case their full-time aspirations do not transpire as planned. Therefore, it is important to remain marketable professionally instead of one-dimensionally.

NON-TRADITIONAL MINISTRY

A false perception exists that once students finish their educational requirements and acquire their ministry credentials, the gates of opportunity will be opened for them. The blood, sweat, and tears they have given to complete their degrees normally yields a diploma and a solid theological foundation that no one can take away, but it does not guarantee of a full-time ministry position. Christian leaders must be open to more

---

121. Ibid.

non-traditional forms of ministry that develop naturally in their neighborhoods and workplaces as they seek to live faithfully and develop relationships in these areas. Additionally, leaders may have to be bi-vocational since compensation for full-time ministry is becoming scarce. Working a "secular" job may also prevent Christian leaders from living in a spiritual bubble. Church ministry tends to isolate Christian leaders from culture. Among the advantages of working in the public domain are increased opportunities to interact with the unchurched on a regular basis.

The positions that provide salary and benefits in a formal church setting are few and far between. The image of serving behind a pulpit and having a nice office from which to manage the church is no longer a realistic option for most Christian leaders. The reality points toward more grassroots and organic forms of service and furthering the Kingdom in their homes, communities, and workplaces. The end goal of formal theological education can no longer be in a full-time pastoral position in a church because this option is an endangered species. The benefit that students will gain from formal theological education is a healthy biblical worldview that they will need as they create their own path and discern where God is calling them to serve as local missionaries. Such options will be less hierarchal and organized and more fluid and loose.

Most likely, their ministries will be birthed in organic ways in the neighborhoods and workplaces they inhabit as they build relationships with the people with whom they live and work. It will require boldness to venture out into the community and develop trust through relationship building, which requires time and effort. They will feel vulnerable while putting themselves out there as local missionaries away from the comfort and protection of the established church. There is no quick fix method of making disciples in this view because it involves a process of being in people's lives over the long run. Since there is no laid-out path to follow, one will need increased reliance and dependency on the Holy Spirit for guidance. Established churches could serve as a valuable support system for those called to incarnational ministries. These local missionaries need the established church to empower their efforts and offer a source of accountability.

Remain Marketable

The idea that a seminary or Bible college degree on a résumé will gain preferential treatment or seem attractive to potential employers in the public domain is a fallacy. In an increasingly secular society, hiring managers are interested in whether the prospective employee can perform the duties of the job. They are interested in the candidate's education and experience required to fulfill the requirements of the position. Though a seminary or Bible college degree may seem attractive to some because of the values Christianity teaches, it will only be secondary to the attributes needed to fulfill the description of the job.

On one occasion, a Christian friend of mine was helping me get a job at her non-profit organization which served the Hispanic community through educational and social programs. She asked me to "secularize" my résumé before she showed it to her boss so she would not be turned off by my religious language. She asked me to emphasize any work experience I had teaching in a public school or any college education preparing me to teach younger kids. Additionally, any applicants who had a teaching certification from the state would be moved to the front of the pile. Unfortunately, most of my teaching experience took place in ministry settings. Even though the hiring manager did consider this experience, it did not hold the same weight and credibility as being state certified. Finding work outside of organizations that are not considered "Christian" is difficult when a student's entire training is geared toward serving inside the local church setting. Employers may have a hard time discerning how the applicant's ministry training and experience could be transferable into a secular company

No Preferential Treatment

I advise my students that a degree from a Bible institute or seminary will not necessarily be attractive to employers. Some may hesitate to hire a student, concerned they will bring their beliefs to work and attempt to convert employees while on the clock. Students should have secular education and experience to work in the marketplace along with a solid biblical foundation to serve incarnationally in society. Above all, an employer's main priority will be in assessing whether applicants have the competencies to perform the job description well. Christian leaders have an opportunity to shine for Jesus working in the various spheres of society, such as government, schools, corporations, hospitals, and so on. For those jobs, of course, they will need the relevant education and experience, but, taking this route, will allow Christian leaders to engage unchurched people on their home turf. A solid theological base will give Christian leaders a biblical worldview, and a missional focus will transform the way the see their purpose in the world as they perform their duties. They will see themselves partnering with God while engaged in society to bring glory to His name.

Who You Know

Another obstacle for paid, full-time ministry positions is the "good ol' boy" system that exists in many established denominations. The few positions that are available are often reserved for those who have deep connections or whose family ties go back generations and can "pull some strings" within the hierarchal structures. Nepotism still exists in the more established organizations as leaders in positions of power favor their close friends and relatives. Additionally, there is greater confidence that the institution will continue to function intact with a candidate who has worked and operated within the system. Family lineage can be the key to maintaining the system of operations that has existed for decades. This also keeps the institution operating the way it always has and any change is met with hostility and resistance. Those with deep ties within the institution will continue the institutional legacy to the next generation. Leaders within the system would rather "go down with the ship" and maintain the status quo than seek to bring much needed transformation. What they do not realize is that the inheritance of ministry the next generation is receiving may not be suitable for a new era if left intact. What future leaders will inherit is a system that is no longer relevant to meet the demands of the changing generations.

Those who are new to the denomination are at a disadvantage to find positions of leadership within the establishment since they do not have deep roots. Many cannot find a support system or mentorship from the establishment to guide them along their leadership journey since many pastors are focused on their own ministries. These established pastors seek to maintain control and positions of authority by placing people to whom they are related. Additionally, the obligations and demands of running their churches leave them little time to be concerned about the future of rising ministers around them. Unfortunately, the extent of their contributions toward rising ministers is limited to what they can contribute to their own ministries. Pastors with an attractional mindset focus their attention on rising leaders if they are contributing to their goals and ambitions.

Many of the Bible students I have taught are left to fend for themselves when trying to make sense of their calling. Their ministry roles usually involve supporting the goals and vision of their pastor and the church. Even though rising leaders can learn tremendously from serving in the local church, time and effort should also be allocated so future generations can fulfill their unique callings in life, which may not necessarily be in the traditional ministry sense, inside the church building. The church should not forget that ministry is not only for the few, but that the body is comprised of many parts, each having an important function. Some may be called to church ministry, but most rising leaders will be working in the public domain as missionaries to their communities and workplaces. The church would be remiss not to properly prepare and support them.

Closing Thoughts

Considering the expansion of an unchurched culture in America, training by churches and seminaries for serving exclusively inside the church building is detrimental to the development of Christian leaders. This style of training is an educational philosophy that was effective in a thriving church culture where a substantial number of persons were seeking out churches to meet their spiritual needs. As the church in general moves from the center of society to the margins, it is necessary to train students to operate out of an exile mindset. To remain relevant, the church must learn to function from the margins of society instead of the center.

For many centuries, pastors were held in high esteem by the broader culture as authority figures with a divine message. At conferences, conventions, and meetings, they were accustomed to being recognized by the majority and given places of honor. They were asked to open various events with prayer, serving as spiritual guides to the general population. They were sought out by political and community leaders for a biblical perspective and divine wisdom on weighty issues.

In today's post-church culture, desiring to go into full-time ministry and pursue formal theological training most likely will not lead to recognition and respect from society. This is no longer something to be expected. Training that emphasizes a more incarnational, exile mindset of ministry, however, will become mandatory to reach communities and workplaces for the gospel. The mentality of "come to us" can no longer be the main evangelistic thrust. Churches and Bible schools would do well to prepare future Christian leaders for serving "in the trenches of culture," with a "go to them" mentality, instead of exclusively serving from within the safety of church buildings.

Biblical Reflection

In 1 Cor. 12:28, the Apostle Paul asserts that some individuals are endowed with the gifts of administration and/or leadership. Even so, it was never his intent to describe those with these gifts as more spiritual and the ones called to do all the heavy lifting within the church. On the contrary, Paul writes, "And [the Holy Spirit] gave some to be apostles, some prophets, some evangelists, and some pastors and teachers" (Eph. 4:11). The functions of the various members of the body are different, but all are essential for the body to operate properly, as the various parts work interdependently to build up the church. Leaders help manage and direct, but they should not be the sole heirs of ministry or be seen to possess a "higher calling" than anyone else. As Paul writes in 1 Cor. 12:14, "For in fact the body is not one member but many." All members of the body serve and build each other up and are then sent out to live faithfully in their communities and workplaces.

A hierarchy of spirituality has created dualistic thinking within the church, where the work in which individuals engage outside of the confines of the church is viewed as secular or less spiritual. Ministry is conceived as serving inside the local church in a program or activity, either full-time or as a volunteer. In such a divided world, Miller explains that occupations in "accounting, carpentry, filmmaking, the arts, farming, and homemaking are secular activities and thus lower activities."[122] He adds that, according to this faulty mentality, "it is best to leave the secular arena and go to into the spiritual arena so we can be 'full-time Christian workers.'"[123]

In the same way that Christ went forth, leaving his residence at the right hand of the Father, the church must leave its turf and become vulnerable in communities and workplaces. By living incarnationally, the laity becomes missionaries to the communities in which members work and live. This gives rise to organically forming ministries on the turf of the unchurched. This approach requires leaders to be intentional about building relationships and sharing their faith as a normal part of life, where most of their time is spent. This leads to whole-life evangelism, where all of one's life becomes a testimony and gives glory to God, through word and deed. Attractional churches are so consumed with programs and activities that they have nothing left to dedicate to building the Kingdom. Attractional churches pull their people into the building and the church agenda to the extent that they become ineffective in their own communities.

WORDS AND PHRASES TO REMEMBER

Professional minister: An individual who has met an array of requirements, such as ordination and seminary training, to serve in a static and attractional posture in a local church. This minister has acquired all the tools necessary to effectively manage and maintain the activities and programs of an attractional church but little to engage culture and society in a missional manner.

---

122. Miller, *Life Work*, 622, Kindle.
123. Ibid., 618.

Spiritual Bubble: As pastors are consumed with the inner organizational requirements of managing a church, they are cutoff from the outside, secular world. They become so absorbed with the inward needs of their churches that they become irrelevant to the broader culture. They live in a spiritual bubble, isolated from society.

KEY VERSES TO REFLECT

1 Cor. 12:14
Eph. 4:11
Mt. 20:28

DISCOVERY QUESTIONS

1. In what ways could you begin to expand your ministry horizons through "outside-the-box" forms of ministry?

2. What Bible verse did you think of when you read this chapter and why?

3. What are some ways you feel you can begin to integrate your faith into the spheres where you spend the bulk of your day (school, neighborhood, workplace)?

4. What resources could you tap into to help you gain greater missional capacity (e.g., books, agencies, training, leaders)?

TRANSITION FOUR

From Compartmentalized to Integrated Life

THE FOURTH TRANSITION INVOLVES BRIDGING the divide between the sacred and secular compartments of life. When the church can close the gap between the sacred and secular, it will be more effective in impacting society in normal, day-to-day activities.

CHAPTER 7

Integrating the Sacred and Secular

━━━◆━━━

LIVING WITH MISSIONAL INTEGRITY

MY WIFE, A PHYSICIAN, STARTED a new phase of training where she specialized in oncology, which focuses on cancer patients. For this new phase, she transitioned to a new hospital and went through orientation her first week. When she came home, she explained how they were going over much of the same material she had learned through medical school and as a resident. She confessed that it was good to be reminded of basic procedures and guidelines as it had been a while since she had covered these. One of the topics they discussed in detail was the idea that physicians could not separate their personal from their professional lives. Who they were at work had to spill over to who they were outside of the hospital. The same professionalism they exhibited in their work environment had to be exemplified in their personal lives.

During orientation, physicians were reminded to be cautious of social media, especially what they posted on Facebook, Twitter, or Instagram. Their social media activity was a direct reflection, not only on them personally, but also on the hospital. Ultimately, physicians cannot separate their lifestyles between what they do at the hospital and what they do away from the hospital. They must exhibit qualities of professionalism wherever they are, even when "off the clock." They were reminded that they were responsible to give the hospital a good name and uphold the values they worked hard to represent. Being a doctor was not something they could put on and take off whenever they felt like it. Physicians are not transformed only by putting on their white coats. The behavior and professionalism that physicians are called to uphold serves as a good illustration for believers, who are called to live with integrity in all realms of life, not only in certain compartments.

LIVING IN COMPARTMENTS

Putting on and taking off one's faith like a garment is hypocritical. Christians are to reflect values that correspond to the teachings of Jesus both at church and away from church, in the "nitty gritty" of life. Scott D. Allen defines integrity as follows:

> To integrate is to coordinate, or blend two or more things into a whole. Integrity means a state of being whole or undivided. Its root world is *integrate*, which is derived from *integer*, "a complete entity." Integrity is often used to describe a quality of character marked by honesty and incorruptibility.[124]

The lack of integration of faith into all realms of life causes compartmentalization, in which "the various spheres begin to function apart from one another."[125] It is easy fall into the practice of separating the Christian life into two separate compartments, especially in a society that is determined to keep religion cut off from the public arena. In the sacred compartment, individuals practice their spiritual duties such as church attendance, Bible study, prayer, worship, and so on. This realm is often mistakenly propped up as the spiritual realm and thus superior to the secular realm. This mental model causes the church grounds to become the center of religious activity, and faith has little or no implications in other areas of one's life. The secular compartment tends to be comprised of life outside of the sacred realm, which is where individuals spend most of their time. The secular realm includes work, school, home, recreation, and civic life.

---

124. Scott D. Allen, *Beyond the Sacred-Secular Divide: A Call to Wholistic Ministry* (Seattle: YWAM, 2011), 43.
125. Callahan, *Effective Church Leadership*, 132.

With a divided mind, individuals attempt to put on different identities that they deem acceptable in the various compartments of life.

Even in work settings, where coworkers know they share the same Christian faith, they may feel pressured to keeping their beliefs a private matter. Companies are increasing their rigidity about employees being open about their faith convictions. In today's increasingly secular society, where employees are discouraged about being open regarding their faith, Christians do not "come out of the closet" for fear of disrupting the stability of the work environment or breaking a company policy. The pressure from a society that is increasingly causing citizens to separate the secular from the sacred is leaving many with a divided mind.

A Divided Mindset

Some of the Bible Institute students I taught expressed how their leadership prohibited member involvement in the men's soccer leagues, claiming to be a "work of the devil," because it keeps individuals from attending church. This only promotes compartmentalization, where, instead of the church being an empowering force for mission, congregational leaders are only fragmenting their people from society. Members are often pulled in numerous directions having to wear different personalities and values in the various spheres of life. Faith fits nicely in the sacred compartment, and churchgoers mark off the religious box by attending Sunday services, participating in Bible studies, and attending Christian conferences. The spiritual box becomes another box to be checked during the week. Many individuals squeeze the religious box into their already hectic schedules, which now competes with their other secular boxes. Each box is fighting for attention and allegiance. Sunday morning serves as the box in which one nourishes the spirit during that brief encounter and God's presence, which is felt acutely during this time. Worshippers begin to see church attendance as a form of therapy for the week so they can cope with the purposelessness and fragmentation of life the rest of the week.

Fellowship becomes the interactions congregants have before and after service. If they are lucky, they can extend fellowship after worship by having lunch at a restaurant. In this brief window of time, individuals experience the best of the spiritual world and the best of fellowship. Church leaders typically hope individuals will be on their best behavior in order to make sure guests feel welcome, worshippers are ministered to, and everyone feels comfortable. For a brief time, churchgoers can avoid the traffic, difficult coworkers, deadlines, and stress that comes with life in the world. Individuals leave Sunday morning service feeling they have done their religious duty for the week and receive a sense of momentary peace and oneness with the divine. According to Gibbs and Bolger, "The modern period created a secular space and relegated spiritual things to the church."[126] A missional mentality would not classify some activities as more spiritual than others but would seek God's guidance in all realms of life. Whether a physician, teacher, pastor, accountant, or any other career, individuals ideally would seek to follow Christ's leading through incarnational initiatives within their work arenas with the hope of the gospel of Christ reaching non-believers through their life.

THE SACRED VS. SECULAR DIVIDE

This compartmentalized framework of faith causes the church grounds and the programs connected with it to become the center of "spirituality." This mindset causes religion to become "both individualized and privatized, to the extent that Christians find themselves living in two largely unrelated worlds"[127] and results in faith having little or no implications in other arenas of one's life. A sense of purpose in matters of faith lies in the hands of the clergy, and their mission is to provide religious goods and services to the attendees. Churchgoers have an opportunity to get away from the "hustle and bustle" of the week and experience a spiritual utopia, at least momentarily. Churchgoers are revitalized through a powerful sermon, anointed worship, and rituals, all of which contribute toward filling their spiritual tanks after being depleted in the absence of the divine the rest of the week. Faith turns into a form of therapy as individuals strive to cope with the difficulties of life. Additionally, individuals may

---

126. Gibbs and Bolger, *Emerging Churches*, 66.
127. Gibbs, *Church Morph*, 50.

feel compelled to attend church when they have a special need or want. Faith becomes individualistic where attendees seek an encounter with the divine to solve their immediate problems, all the while not realizing that they are also called to a life of mission.

The secular compartments are unspiritual and tend to be comprised of the spheres of life outside of the sacred realm, yet this is where individuals spend most of their time. In this compartmentalized view, Christian Scharen opines that faith becomes "at best one piece of a busy life, perhaps impacting one's 'soul' or 'heart,'" and "as a means to help cope with the hectic pace of the rest of life, where other values rule."[128] As people go about their week in their communities and workplaces, faith becomes a box to check off along with the other boxes of life the rest of the week. As people of faith transition between boxes, they feel forced to put on a different persona that corresponds to the values associated with any given box. Christians feel compelled to "check their faith at the door" to find acceptance in these secular arenas. In some more hostile environments, such as the public school system, which is continuously attempting to distance itself from particular faith groups, teachers have resorted to "losing one's religion" in order to avoid being ostracized as a religious fanatic.

At church, Christians feel a sense of relief because they are given permission to wear their religious hats freely. Integration is becoming more and more difficult as the gap between church and state gets wider in America and society moves from being a basically Christian nation to a pluralistic one. As mentioned earlier, in Houston, Texas, there are more than 93 languages spoken on any given day and over 120 nations represented. Along with this diversity comes a stream of different religious expressions. To avoid confrontations, society in general has decided to avoid showing any preferential treatment toward any one faith group. To avoid religious conflict, American society has resorted to separating the workforce from faith altogether.

---

128. Christian B. Scharen, *Faith as a Way of Life: A Vision for Pastoral Leadership* (Grand Rapids: Eerdmans, 2008), 15.

Each box has its own independent value system that requires individuals to change their identities to get along in any given environment. The spiritual box has its own value system that is kept separate, and elements of the religious arena are met with resistance when individuals attempt to integrate its values into other boxes. The rejection and discomfort Christians feel of making their faith public forces them to keep their faith private to avoid the tension. Where there is less freedom to express one's beliefs, Christians may have to use subtle, non-expressive forms to share their faith. Whenever the opportunity arises, however, believers should not shy away from boldly sharing the gospel with others.

INCREASED SOCIETAL REJECTION

American society, in becoming increasingly secular in the public domain, further forces individuals to keep their faith a personal matter for fear of the consequences. Companies and institutions are implementing policies about sharing one's faith with customers and coworkers. This causes Jesus to become "my personal Savior" and individuals keep their beliefs private not to make waves. For this reason, churches and Bible colleges should incorporate missional training, which will be crucial as Christians learn to navigate in a post-Christian society as local missionaries. The same specialized training that missionaries receive before going overseas into hostile territory should be the new normal for congregants in the local churches. The American church continues to operate as if it still at the center of society and falsely believes that is can be passive about reaching the nations for Christ. With the incorporation of missional training, average Joes and Janes will begin to see themselves as local missionaries sent to their communities and workplaces.

Instead, Christians are being pressured to live divided minds on both fronts. When they are in the public domain, they feel pressure to renounce their faith, and when they are at church they feel pressure to disassociate with activities that are deemed secular or unspiritual. Missionaries to Zanzibar, a country in Africa that is 90% Muslim and hostile to Christianity, are scrutinized by local authorities to make sure they are only teaching English and not attempting to share the gospel in the classroom. Though Zanzibar may feel like a far cry from what is happening in mainstream society in America, the resistance that Christians are facing locally is increasingly feeling more and more like Zanzibar in the public sphere. This is especially true considering the plurality of beliefs in American society and the religious tensions that are increasing in the public domain.

For this reason, ordinary Christians leading regular lives need to operate more like overseas missionaries. Considering the increasingly diverse and global population that is represented in the U.S., the American church should be learning from overseas missionaries how to infiltrate hostile territory. Since America seems to be losing ground on being a Christian nation, believers can no longer operate from a position of influence. There once was a time in America where most citizens went to a Christian church on Sunday. It was completely reasonable to think that the majority of one's neighbors and coworkers were Christians. Now, it is not uncommon in most urban communities to have neighbors living on the same street who are atheists, Muslims, and Buddhists, as well as other faith traditions.

A THEORY FOR COMPARTMENTALIZATION

There are multifaceted reasons for explaining how compartmentalization has influenced the American church. One phenomenon has its origins in the agrarian society of the 1930s when the U.S. had vast, open spaces. Family units had lots of land, so their survival depended on raising animals and planting crops. Most families were separated from other families for miles, and visiting others often involved several days of travel on horseback or carriage. This forced family units to form their own miniature societies where they could meet all their needs independently without any outside help. Life revolved around the farm and the land. Slowly, as the population in these areas increased, dependency on others also rose. Families had to learn to rely on one another more and more, which made life much easier. These communities were built on "neighborly reciprocity,"[129] as described by Christian B. Scharen. As growth continued, people began to specialize

---

129. Scharen, *Faith as a Way of Life*, 16.

in the different spheres of society, providing more vocational options from which to choose. New spheres of society began to take shape in religion, politics, economics, recreation, and education.

In an agrarian society, farming and raising animals were the primary vocations. In the 21st century, there are thousands of occupational codes available to American workers. Colleges and universities train and educate citizens to fill all these roles, which is in stark contrast to an agrarian society where education was only offered to children at home by their parents. Eventually, children were taught in a one-room schoolhouse where all ages were taught together. Students did not have an incentive to go past the 5th grade since there was only one line of work available to them. Today, there are a plethora of available options in education, and it has become extremely specialized, offering "preschool, kindergarten, elementary and intermediate school, middle school, high school, college, vocational schools, technological schools, graduate schools, postgraduate schools, and continuing education."[130] Even within each category, there are subspecialties like Montessori, private, Christian, bi-lingual, college prep, and so on.

Self-Protection

Population density created more vocational opportunities in education and the same became true in other spheres. As vocational specialization increased in politics, economics, recreation, religion, and so on, these various spheres cut off from one another. What started as one society confined to the family unit morphed into multiple spheres of society that rarely interact or communicate with one another, resulting in societal alienation. In the words of Callahan, "Each sphere begins to function as though it were the whole."[131] Additionally, they are all equally competing for the loyalty, resources, and energy of the citizens of society, creating a highly competitive atmosphere. Each sphere sees itself as superior and fails to see outside of itself and toward the interconnectedness within society. Any

---

130. Callahan, *Effective Church Leadership*, 128.
131. Callahan, *Effective Church Leadership*, 132.

collaboration that develops is based solely on the benefits other partners will provide in helping achieve organizational goals. Once a partner's usefulness is depleted, the bond between them is broken.

A Competitive Climate

As each sphere in society becomes preoccupied with its own agenda and objectives, a competitive atmosphere is created with each fighting for allegiance from the same pool of citizens, further distancing themselves from one another. Unfortunately, this tendency is also evident in the religious sphere among churches. Just like everyone else, churches find themselves fighting for the loyalty, time, and energy of their local community's citizens. Each church becomes self-absorbed with its own progress and survival, so that each one creates its own little subculture that is distanced from society. As the church's relevance in a post-church culture diminishes, it is tempted to take on a protective posture, cultivating a culture of self-centeredness and territorialism.

The self-protective stance easily transforms the church into the "attractional" mode. Its main objective is internal functioning: programs, budget, building, and attendance. Its main strategy becomes getting people in through the doors, which means convincing others to change their allegiances from other spheres of society and favoring the religious sphere. The attractional church measures it success by numerical growth—butts in the seats and balances in the bank accounts. The focus is on material progress, not service, money, or mission. People are used as commodities to achieve the church's goals and objectives. As managers, pastors run their churches more like businesses than as outposts for mission to a broken and hurting world.

Missional Leadership

Clearly, churches and Bible colleges need to shift away from this ineffective, compartmentalized model and move toward an integrated, missional model of ministry. Instead of increasing compartmentalization and isolation, "the missionary pastor helps to build bridges in all spheres of the culture,"[132] according to Callahan. The integration of multiple arenas of life is one of the special tasks of a missional leader. When I taught at a Bible institute, my task was to develop missional leaders. The hope was that these rising leaders would begin to live integrated lives for themselves in society, encourage the same whole life discipleship principles in others, and then scatter to serve in the different spheres of society.

Leaders lead in the same way that they are led. If training can instill missional principles in their life encouraging integrity of faith, they will do the same with others under their care and leadership. Gibbs and Bolger have described this skill set as "sacralization, the process of making all of life sacred,"[133] which unites the Kingdom with all aspects of life so they run together, not separate. In the following, Callahan describes the challenge for leaders to live amid the world, not apart from it:

> The task is best done as missionary pastors launch and lead intentional missional groupings that bridge various spheres of the culture. The art is to identify a specific human hurt and hope and deliver concrete, effective help in all spheres of the culture. One thus attacks the human hurt in a holistic way, not a compartmentalized way. In the process, the missionary pastor helps build bridges in all spheres of the culture. The task is not easy.[134]

Through integration of faith into all realms of life, the church can slow the trend of its irrelevancy. Gibbs and Bolger describe this division of the sacred and secular realms as the creation of "a bubble in the surrounding water."[135] It is essential for missional leaders in post-Christendom to redefine the sacred versus secular compartments of life. The church cannot afford to live in its own isolated spiritual bubble if it hopes to impact the surrounding culture with the gospel. This dualistic thought finds its origins in Hellenism, the result of which, for Frost and Hirsch,

---

132. Callahan, *Effective Church Leadership*, 136.
133. Gibbs and Bolger, *Emerging Churches*, 66.
134. Callahan, *Effective Church Leadership*, 136.
135. Gibbs and Bolger, *Emerging Churches*, 67.

is that it creates a "schism between sacred and secular so fundamental to Christendom modes of thinking."[136] Such sacred versus secular thinking perpetuates the church having an exclusively attractional posture. This mindset believes that service to the Lord is rendered inside the church and its programs and anything outside or contrary to this is less valuable or secondary.

The attractional church has not done the body of Christ any favors in helping congregants seek greater integrity. When the church focuses on its agenda and becomes blind to the mission toward the community-at-large, this mindset is transmitted to the body. The congregation becomes the buyer of the spiritual goods and services the church offers, which are dispensed by the few ministry experts on staff. The bulk of the resources the church has available go to meeting the needs of the congregation, creating nominal Christians that are forever dependent on the professional ministers. This clergy-laity divide keeps the ordinary Christian stagnant, constantly learning but hardly growing. Most of the energy of the attractional church is directed inward, losing sight of the essence of why the church exists. This self-absorption causes a wall of separation between the sacred and the secular realms of life.

HOLISTIC MINISTRY

Frost and Hirsch describe this Western spiritual tradition as unbiblical, stating that "there is no distinction whatsoever between the secular and the sacred in the Hebrew worldview. All of life is sacred when it is placed in relationship to the living God. The Hebraic mind can draw a direct line from any and every aspect of life to the eternal purposes of God."[137] The Scriptures are utterly holistic, which Allen describes as "the idea that the parts of a whole must be understood in relationship to the whole. It emphasizes the whole and the interdependence of the parts rather than the parts in and of themselves."[138] The objective was to instill

---

136. Frost and Hirsch, *The Shaping of Things to Come*, 127.
137. Frost and Hirsch, *The Shaping of Things to Come*, 126.
138. Allen, *Beyond the Sacred-Secular Divide*, 18-19.

whole life discipleship, which is all-inclusive, extending "to all aspects of our lives, including our families, vocations, studies, leisure activities, and daily routines."[139]

The lives of Christians in their entirety should bring forth an evangelistic message. The students I taught were probably not expecting this class to have gone in this direction. The mental models they had developed on evangelism were ingrained, and understanding these principles was not intuitive. Yet, I knew that at least one student in my class was connecting the dots. When he sent me an article by Daniel Darling titled "A Call to the Cubicle," I knew I was reaching at least one person, and I saw it as a huge victory. The concept, "There is no division between the sacred and secular, the whole earth is the Lord's, including the places we work,"[140] was beginning to alter this student's mental framework.

The concept of a holistic life opposes dualism, where Christians fall into the trap of leading a divided life. Dualism leads to a separation between the spiritual, made up of faith, worship, and church involvement, and secular, made up of family, careers, and recreation. When believers live with integrity, their faith impacts all spheres of life, not only certain compartments. Acquiring greater integration in life will promote a better understanding of individual roles in the Kingdom of God as believers become more intentional about impacting spheres of influence in neighborhoods and communities. This is especially critical in a culture with growing hostility toward Christianity that rejects the notion that the church is an authority to be heard and followed.

Integrating the Sacred and Secular

The secular and sacred divide will hinder the church from impacting culture. In this view, individuals experience spiritual life during the times they participate in the functions and activities connected with the church. The rest of the time, they are passive and unable to find religious significance beyond the church grounds where they spend most of

---

139. Ibid., 33.
140. Daniel Darling, "A Call to the Cubicle," *En Contacto*, accessed Sept. 1, 2015, http://encontacto.org/lea/revista/fe-obras/un-llamado-al-cubiculo.

their time. Life outside of the sacred realm is considered to be the secular realm where matters of faith convictions fail to be lived out daily. In Frost's words, "We can easily think of a friend entering church-ordained ministry as following God, but rarely do we speak of a decision to become a computer programmer or a nurse or a filmmaker or an accountant as similarly following God's calling in our lives."[141] Figure 1 shows the dualistic nature of some Christians and how it is easy to separate the sacred and secular compartments of life. To be missional, Christians need to integrate their faith into the secular realm without losing their distinctiveness.

Figure 1. Integrating Faith and Life to Avoid Compartmentalization

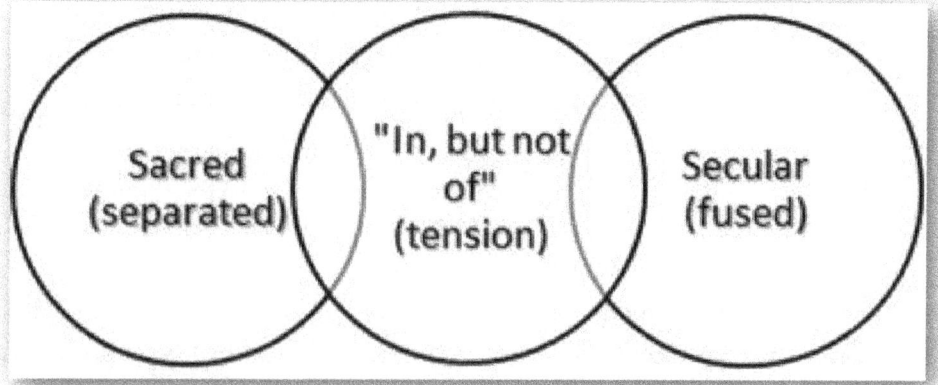

The heart of the course, prepared for Hispanic Bible students, was to confront a dualistic worldview that pervades the church and separates the various spheres of life into either "spiritual and physical or religious and secular."[142] The lack of integration of faith into all realms of life causes compartmentalization, in which "the various spheres begin to function apart from one another."[143] In the sacred compartment, individuals tend to practice their spiritual duties such as church attendance, Bible study, prayer, worship, and so on. This realm is often seen as superior or more

---

141. Frost, *Exiles: Living Missionally in a Post-Christian Culture*, 185.
142. Miller, *LifeWork*, 675, Kindle.
143. Callahan, *Effective Church Leadership*, 132.

spiritual than the secular realm. This mental model causes the church grounds to become the center of religious activity and faith has few implications in other areas of one's life. Miller describes this as evangelical Gnosticism, meaning the split between the spiritual and physical or worldly that exists within evangelical Protestantism. Gnosticism stems from ancient Greek philosophy, with many of the ideas attributed to Plato. He divided "creation into two self-existing and eternal parts: the spiritual was considered superior, while the material was inferior."[144] In his book, *Beyond the Sacred-Secular Divide*, Allen attempts to address this division and helps readers find faith integration in the following excerpt:

> But God is at work today, leading a generation back to an undivided understanding of the kingdom of God and the earth. What lies beyond the secular-sacred divide? A fulfilling, integrated life that unites faith and action, the spiritual and the physical, Sundays and the rest of the week. God cares about every part, and we have to the incredible opportunity to join him in his all-encompassing, redemptive plan for our world. What are we waiting for?[145]

God is seeking "to reconcile all things to himself" (Col. 1:19-20), and Christians are to intentionally seek to live all of life in God's presence, including work, home, ministry, and recreation. When Jesus says, "follow me" (Mk. 8:34), he wants people of faith to live faithfully in all spheres of life, not only when it is easy or beneficial. There are no activities that are more spiritual than others under this view. This perspective of evangelism goes against a dualistic view of the message of salvation as merely "saving souls for heaven." Also, under this view, the priority of the church is not narrowed to the number of decisions made or the number of individuals attending an evangelistic outing. When convincing outsiders to become insiders by attending one of the scheduled church services become paramount, salvation ceases to be one of the main thrusts of evangelism.

---

144. Allen, *Beyond the Sacred-Secular Divide*, 97.
145. Ibid. Excerpt taken from the back of the book.

Following the way of Jesus, a missional perspective emphasizes whole life discipleship, which becomes a way of life in all spheres, not only in certain compartments.

CORAM DEO

Miller uses the Latin phrase *coram Deo* to describe the integrative, holistic posture that Christians should take as they go about their daily tasks. This phrase is defined as "before the face of God,"[146] referring to the lifestyle in which Christians are called to surrender all their compartments to the Lordship of Christ. The evangelistic message they preach does not only come out of their mouths but it is the message they give through their lives. In this sense, worship is not confined to what happens during corporate gatherings. Worship becomes more than just raising one's arms and following the direction of the worship leaders on stage. Instead, worship becomes honoring God and praising him through lives of service to others. The words of Francis of Assisi, "Preach the gospel and if you have to, use words," are reminders that the message we give with our lives matters as much as the words we speak. This view takes evangelism one step further to avoid compartmentalizing it as another event connected to the local church instead of a way of life. It is a lifestyle to live missionally, evangelize naturally, and worship throughout one's daily life, giving glory to God in every sphere of life, not only during certain times of the week.

CULTURAL ENGAGEMENT

Culture is multi-layered, comprising people's experiences, backgrounds, and upbringings. Culture also provides a platform on which to exercise creativity in the arts, literature, and music. Culture gives people a sense of identity when they can identify with their ethnic customs, traditions, and language. Culture is also comprised of more complex systems in society such as education, government, health, and religion. These are institutions essential to culture that give societies a sense of order and stability. Along with healthy aspects of culture, evil forces are also imbedded in culture.

---

146. Miller, *Life Work*, loc 1404, Kindle.

For these principalities and powers to be confronted, the church needs to be dispersed—leave its bubble—and engage culture on its home turf. If left unchecked, these principalities will cause isolation, stunt human progress, and diminish human dignity. The church is sent out and dispersed in various spheres of public life to engage culture in a way that the light of gospel will be shed in the darkness. The church tends to engage culture on a range between two poles: One pole is being antagonistic toward culture; the other is being assimilated into culture so that the church loses its salt and is useless.

Cultural Antagonism

As stated, there are two extremes in engaging culture. One is antagonistic (against) and the other is accommodationist (for).[147] The first view takes everything about culture and labels it as bad and under demonic dominion, to be avoided at all costs. This approach is seen in the church when it has completely isolated itself and created its own Christian subculture to protect itself from the evil influences of the world. The church is so afraid of being tainted that it lives in its own little bubble, separated from the world. Richard Niebuhr notes, "Loyalty to Christ and the brothers is the rejection of cultural society; a clear line of separation is drawn between the brotherhood of the children of God (Church) and the world."[148] This us-versus-them mentality creates a wall of separation between the church and the world. The church becomes distant to the degree that it becomes utterly irrelevant and impotent regarding the ability to make a difference in society. Mistakenly, in its attempt to keep itself from being tainted, the church creates a Christian subculture that blocks itself off from culture. Consequently, evangelism has been devolved into an attempt to extract people from their communities and get them across into the religious zone. As such, the sacred versus secular mentality blocks off the church from society and perpetuates the church having an exclusively attractional posture.

---

147. H. Richard Niebuhr, *Christ & Culture* (San Francisco: HarperCollins Publishers, 1951), xlv.
148. Niebuhr, *Christ & Culture*, 47-48.

Cultural Accommodation

The second unhealthy way to engage culture is to assimilate into the culture to the degree that Christians lose their distinctiveness. This extreme makes it difficult to differentiate Christian values and the distorted values of the world. Rah explains this extreme as "the Church and culture are not in conflict," and "culture becomes a way to discover God."[149] This approach seeks to embrace everything that culture offers and strives to find harmony between culture and the gospel. A church member under this framework may frequent bars and clubs to reach the lost. In this enmeshed attempt to reach the world, he might end up getting drunk and involved in an inappropriate sexual relationship, thus negating his witness. This example may seem extreme, but the point is that the world is influencing the church more than the church is influencing the world. This effect may happen on a broader scale, where a society's culture has influenced the church like what has happened with the pull of consumerism or materialism. The two extremes of being either antagonistic toward or accommodated into culture attempt to pull the church apart. The church either separates itself from the world out of fear, becoming irrelevant, or assimilates into the world, taking on the distorted values of culture without any discretion. Each church is somewhere on the spectrum and needs to monitor its balance carefully between the two so it does not fall into deeply onto one side. The church must seek to maintain the tension of being in the world but not of the world. Otherwise, it will lose its saltiness and distinctiveness, and the world will find it difficult to make a distinction between the followers of Christ and the unchurched.

A Balanced Approach

Walls between the church and society have the potential to inhibit Christians from effectively influencing culture in a positive manner. Christians are not to abandon and forsake the world entirely and build a version of Noah's ark where only one family gets saved. Under this

---

149. From a class with Professor Soong-Chan Rah at Houston Graduate School of Theology. Among others, one of his books is *Many Colors: Cultural Intelligence for a Changing Church*.

antagonistic posture, any engagement in society involves throwing out a life jacket and reeling people into the boat. People on the boat are safe and secure if they stay onboard and avoid getting out. On the flipside, Christians must not seek to find harmony with the world just to stay in good relationship, ignoring when its values are anti-kingdom. Those characterized as the "salt of the earth" are not to make a home with culture to the extent that it will become tasteless and thrown out. Prayerful consideration should be taken when evaluating the values and principles of culture as Christians discern when to reject, accept, engage, withdraw, transform, and even stay neutral, all the while living in the world and remaining faithful the Christ.

There are two extremes in Niebuhr's model and each of us falls somewhere on or in between these extremes in different situations. As Christians go about their lives, they must discern aspects of culture that are acceptable, others that should be rejected, and even remain neutral in some situations. Additionally, Christ may call Christians to participate with him to bring transformation and redemption to an area. Considering the streams of change in the 21st century, there is no longer a one-size-fits-all method of engagement with the ebb and flow of culture. Believers are called to be "salt and light" in society (Mt. 5: 13-16), which implies they are to be in the world and engaged in society. Additionally, the Apostle Paul urges the church to "come out from them and be separate from them . . . and touch nothing unclean" (2 Cor. 6: 17). With these mixed messages, there are no easy answers for how Christians can best engage culture. There is no one solution that applies to all situations or one recipe that is the "high road" in all circumstances. Niebuhr's model demonstrates the array of perspectives that Christians can adopt, which, when combined with prayer and Bible study, hopefully will lead toward a faithful course of action.

Some churches have nurtured an individualistic, one-dimensional response to the gospel, emphasizing "personal salvation, individual conversion, and incorporation into the church,"[150] but they have no framework for

---

150. Mortimer Arias, *Announcing the Reign of God: Evangelization and the Subversive Memory of Jesus* (Eugene Or: Wipf & Stock, 1984), xv.

holistic ministry that addresses the broader brokenness in society. They need an understanding of the Hebrew word *shalom*, which "embraces all dimensions of human life: physical, spiritual, personal and interpersonal, communal and societal, historical and eternal."[151] Similarly, a holistic view of salvation "encompasses all human relationship—with the neighbor, with nature, and with God."[152]

Closing Remarks

The church is uniquely positioned to find a balance between "the life of God's people gathered, the *ekklesia*, [and] the church dispersed in the world, the *diaspora*, in marketplace, government, professional offices, schools and home."[153] Worship is not only confined to corporate gatherings where the laity are passively engaged as spectators. The laity is often reduced to receive religious goods and services while only a few professional ministers are authorized to be dispensers. In this view, worship is limited to a set hour during Sunday service with limited implications the rest of the week. Instead, worship should extend out from the formal gathering site to the rest of life. The laity can become the hands and feet of Jesus through the ordinary rhythms and patterns of life. As the laity engages society, God will be glorified through lives presented as living sacrifices in the trenches of society, which is their reasonable service (Rom. 12:2).

Christians will have their faith put to the test as they begin to live their lives with greater integrity. Taking up the cross in all areas of life, not only when it is easy or convenient, is not easy. Putting on different personalities as one sees fit becomes defined as lukewarm Christianity. Christians are to "lose their life so they can find it," which requires them to live boldly for Christ in the trenches of society. There is no single formula or recipe to faithfully pursue "making disciples of all nations." A key aspect of missional training encourages integrating one's various compartments of life to achieve greater integrity among them. Bridging the gap between the

---

151. Ibid.
152. Arias, *Announcing the Reign of God*, xv.
153. Stevens, *The Other Six Days*, 65, Kindle.

compartments the church has categorized as either sacred or secular will promote a whole-life culture of discipleship. Often, individuals "wear different hats," and when they exit one area of life, they put on another hat for the area they are entering. When individuals begin to integrate their homes, neighborhoods, and work, they wear fewer hats because their status as a missionary does not change depending on where they are at any given time. Their faith and the calling of God on their lives follows them everywhere as they go and make disciples, dispersing throughout society.

BIBLICAL INSIGHTS

One major positive of being conquered by Babylon is that Israel's exilic state rejuvenated their missional existence. Beach writes, "Exile brought about a renewed sense that Israel had a role to play among the nations of the world in declaring the supremacy of Yahweh."[154] In Babylon, Israel was supposed to be a countercultural society, a witness to the people they resented and feared. This could only be done by integrating and assimilating themselves into the culture. The prophet Jeremiah writes to the exiles, "Your *shalom* will be found in Babylon's *shalom*" (Jer. 29:11). Israel was to be a witness to God's compelling vision of the Hebrew word *shalom*, which is translated "peace" in English but has a comprehensive and multi-faceted understanding in the Old Testament. "That persistent vision of joy, well-being, harmony, and prosperity," Brueggemann writes, "is not captured in a single word or idea in the Bible, and a cluster of words is required to express its many dimensions and subtle nuances: love, loyalty, truth, grace, salvation, blessing, righteousness."[155] As it had always been for them, Israel was the manifestation of God's presence and the means by which Yahweh initiated his vision in Babylon. Even in an exiled state, the glory of Yahweh was made manifest through his people, a light to the nations as they lived out their faith in their neighborhoods, workplaces, market, and homes. They would be witnesses and agents of

---

154. Beach, *The Church in Exile*, 808, Kindle.
155. Walter Brueggemann, *Living Toward a Vision* (Philadelphia: United Church Press, 1982), 23, 15-16.

peace and prosperity, bringing glory to God in a pagan land through their lives. While under dominion, Israel was to manifest God's presence and peace through their lifestyle.

Words and Phrase to Remember

Sacred/Secular Divide: Life is divided into two realms. In the sacred compartment, individuals practice their spiritual duties such as church attendance, Bible study, prayer, worship, and so on. This realm is often seen as superior or more spiritual to the secular realm. The secular realm is the sphere of work, school, recreation, and civic life.

Life Integration: The integration of Christian faith and service into all realms of life, instilling whole-life discipleship. Christian witness extends into all aspects of life, including the family unit, the workplace, school, civic life, leisure activities, and daily routines.

Wholism: In Allen's words, "the idea that the parts of a whole must be understood in relationship to the whole. It emphasizes the whole and the interdependence of the parts rather than the parts in and of themselves."[156]

Key Scripture to Reflect

Jer. 29:11
Col. 1:19-20
Mt. 5:13-16

Discovery Questions

1. What are some areas of your life where you feel are divided between the sacred and secular?

---

156. Allen, *Beyond the Sacred-Secular Divide*, 18-19.

2. List two ways you can begin to integrate the compartment of your life and find increased missional integrity.

3. List two specific examples where you need to held the tension between "being in the world, but not of the world."

CHAPTER 8

Faith and Vocation

SECULAR VS. SACRED CALLINGS

> The pastor announced, "John has resigned from his lucrative career in business and will start working in full-time ministry. Now he works for Christ." The congregation burst out in praise and cheer, but my heart became sad and I felt embarrassed for the man seated next to me. He was my father, a good entrepreneur, who had not left his business to start to work full-time in the work of the Lord.[157]

THE STORY ABOVE CAME FROM an article a student sent to me after a discussion on vocation in class at the Bible Institute where I was teaching. It is an all too familiar story of a church pastor erroneously perceiving secular work as a step down in comparison to working in full-time ministry. Careers in business, education, law, customer service, and other fields are often not considered to be areas with a potential to impact others and as fertile ground for ministry. The word "ministry" is usually correlated with full-time work in a church setting. Paid staff members in churches are in ministry, but others who have careers outside of the church setting have secular jobs. Those not in full-time ministry, however, have an opportunity to do ministry a few hours during the week. Typically, this part-time ministry work is when they are at their church serving in some

---

157. Darling, "A Call to the Cubicle."

capacity--as a Sunday school teacher, usher, sound system tech, or any other service on church grounds.

Unfortunately, this story is a common occurrence in today's church subculture where there are tiers of ministry. Some vocations are worthy to be acknowledged as working for the Lord, while others are mere secular jobs. Even though the entrepreneur in the article had been a pillar for his congregation for many years, his work as a Christian business owner was not recognized as ministry even when he was having a profound impact on his employees. Often, individuals who work in business or another secular career are seen, primarily, as the financial backers or volunteers for the church's goals and projects. The impact these individuals may have in their communities or workplaces are often not considered ministry and rarely acknowledged, since these may not further the church's plans and purposes.

In contrast, the concept that "there is no division between the sacred and secular, the whole earth is the Lord's, including the places we work"[158] is a premise that should be promoted and encouraged within the church. With a divided mindset, church leaders easily fail to cultivate a perspective among their congregants where they begin to see themselves as missionaries and ministers sent out to the world, outside of the confines of the church. These are the spheres where they have significant influence and can serve as God's representatives being salt and light to a broken world.

Marketplace Ministry

Approximately fifty percent of the awake time of Americans is spent at work,[159] making the marketplace is an excellent opportunity for incarnational ministry. For this reason, it would make sense for workplaces to be where missional leaders begin to integrate the secular and sacred compartments of life. It is not only the place where American workers spend most of their time but where meaningful relationships are naturally built. Churches and Christian colleges that desire to work at broadening

---

158. Darling, "A Call to the Cubicle."
159. Bureau of Labor Statistics, "American Time Use Survey," accessed Aug. 21, 2014, http://www.bls.gov/tus/charts/chart1.pdf.

the range of possibilities for Kingdom service might consider deterring aspiring ministers from holding a narrow view of ministry as primarily full-time devotion to the church building and its members. Especially in a post-church culture where full-time positions as congregational pastors are growing scarcer every day, Christian leaders would do well to include the workplace as a mission field and emphasize the essential role the Christian workforce can have in the public realm. This integrated thinking helps prepare Christian leaders to be incarnational by engaging the unchurched in the marketplace. This intentional planning prevents the tendency of the attractional model to create compartments that separate the secular from the sacred in the world.

The goal of placing full-time ministry at the pinnacle of service is no longer an option for the majority. The time is approaching for Bible college and seminary students to view secular jobs as viable paths to make a difference for the sake of the Kingdom, particularly as America becomes more secularized. Construction workers, engineers, customer service reps, and teachers can experience transformative relationships and interactions that are just as important for the Kingdom as serving in a full-time capacity in a church setting. As a matter of fact, Christians who work in the public domain have more constant contact with the unchurched and are better positioned to serve as ambassadors bridging a relationship with Christ. Then, exercising one's calling in the workplace will not be perceived as a step down from full-time ministry. Full-time church leaders cannot reach the unchurched in the marketplace like the congregants can while working in the public arena. The reach of the church can be extended significantly when church leaders create a culture within the congregation that emphasizes the workplace as the mission field in which the laity is sent to make disciples and build bridges.

PLAN B

When I taught at a Bible institute, most of the students were aspiring pastors and ministers. Many were hoping to become full-time pastors since this is what working in ministry meant to them. Even though aspiring to this position is a respected endeavor, I emphasize the need for them to have a Plan B in case their aspirations of working in full-time ministry do not develop exactly as they envision. I never discourage students to avoid pursuing full-time ministry because some may be called to serve in this capacity, but I caution them about the availability of these paid positions. I attempted to be realistic about their hopes and aspirations. I have seen too many times how fathers and mothers have put their families in perilous situations because they felt called to ministry and decided to cut off all sources of secular income completely.

In one example, things got so bad financially for a family seeking full-time ministry that they accepted the invitation from another family to live in their two- bedroom apartment, making a total of ten people in this apartment. It put both families in an awkward bind, and, at the end, they were asked to leave, which resulted in feelings of shame and grief. Having a Plan B in this circumstance could have brought huge relief to the ousted family. I tell this story to be truthful about those seeking full-time, paid positions and how important it is that those aspiring to these positions know that they are not guaranteed. More importantly, I endeavor to expand their horizons on what they may perceive as working for the Lord. This is one way to help students and younger people develop a new vision for ministry.

THE MEANING OF WORK

Hugh Whelchel has promoted and written extensively on the biblical perspective of work, specifically on the type that is normally not considered to be full-time ministry. In his book, *How Then Should We Work? Rediscovering the Biblical Doctrine of Work*, he provides a primer on integrating faith and work. He seeks to encourage the church to view vocation from a biblical viewpoint and strives to dismantle the idea that full-time ministry is considered a higher calling or more spiritual when compared to work outside the confines of the church building, in the secular world. The work accomplished in secular vocations can have deep meaning and purpose when fulfilled with a Kingdom worldview. This view has the potential to transform people's lives as they seek God's purposes at work, the place they spend the bulk of their time. Whelchel writes:

> Few, however, understand that even in our everyday work, the Scripture teaches no separation between the secular and sacred. No church-related work or mission is more spiritual than any other profession such as law, business, education, journalism, or politics. All of our actions should be unified in obedience to God and for God's glory (1 Cor. 10:31; Col. 3:17). The Kingdom of God bears on every dimension of life, and agents of the Kingdom serve as salt and light (Mt. 5:13-16) wherever the Spirit leads them.[160]

As stated above, approximately fifty percent of the waking hours of average Americans are spent at work. Unfortunately, work is often a means to an end instead of a place where Kingdom service can be accomplished. There is much biblical support for whole-life discipleship, in which all spheres of life are to be under the Lordship of Christ (Mt. 28:18; Col. 1:17; Heb. 1:3). Since work plays a vital role in people's lives, taking up most of their time, there is no sense to view work only as the means to a paycheck. Work can provide immense amounts of meaning and purpose if viewed as an avenue to expand God's Kingdom in the world. Especially considering the statistic that "77% of Americans hate their job,"[161] if workplace could be viewed with a Kingdom lens and a place where individuals can impact society, there would be much less hatred toward going into work in the morning.

Churchgoers, who have not thought of their ordinary life as a place for fulfilling their Kingdom purpose, should consider a paradigm shift. Lay members, who are not considered full-time ministers, should see themselves as unpaid missionaries in the public domain, playing an active, full-time

---
160. Hugh Whelchel, *How Then Should We Work? Rediscovering the Biblical Doctrine of Work* (Bloomington, IN: Westbow Press, 2012) 2, Kindle.
161. Hugh Whelchel, *How Then Should We Work*, 336, Kindle.

role as a volunteer in reigning in God's Kingdom. Simultaneously, the paid clergy should be intentional in helping the ordinary person see that part-time ministries extend beyond the church walls. Often, the church divides God's people into those who do ministry and those to whom it is done. If the laity could begin to see their paid work environment as their volunteer mission field, it could prompt "a life dedication to being part of God's plan for creation and liberation,"[162] as Roy Lewis puts it. Through any given line of work, people of faith can feel a sense of calling where they can join God in his redemptive plan. The workplace has enormous potential for ministry where ordinary people can begin to function as local missionaries in the often hardest to reach spheres of life.

VOCATION

Understanding the word "vocation" can help the church more fully pursue the vision of believers seeing the marketplace as an area to bring wholeness to the brokenness in the world. According to William Placher, when the Bible speaks of call or vocation, "it characteristically means a call to faith or to do a special task in God's service."[163] Whelchel further distinguishes primary from secondary vocations, stating that an individual's primary vocation is "a call to faith in Christ (Rom. 8:28-30; 1 Cor. 1:9), a call to the Kingdom of God (1 Thess. 2:10-12)."[164] Secondary vocations manifest themselves by serving God's purposes in "our work in the world."[165] Work, therefore, will no longer be seen solely as a means to an end, but the place where Christians can join God in his Kingdom purposes. Especially since work is the place where people spend the bulk of their time, this can also be the place where they can have considerable influence. The workplace is where fruitful ministry can take place, which can give believers

---

162. Roy Lewis, *Choosing Your Career, Finding Your Vocation: A Step-by Step Guide for Adults and Counselors* (New York: Paulist Press, 1989), 38.
163. William Placher, ed., *Callings: Twenty Centuries of Christian Wisdom on Vocation* (Grand Rapids: Eerdmans, 2005), 4.
164. Whelchel, *How Then Should We Work*, 5, Kindle.
165. Ibid.

a profound sense of purpose, knowing they are sent as ambassadors on a mission to affect change in this arena of life.

Carrying Out His Purposes

The calling to a relationship with Christ manifests itself through a transformed life, which naturally spills over to an individual's vocation. Scorgie describes this as "actively participating in God's purposes in the world (139)." God calls his people to carry out his purposes and plans for humanity in "a particular line of work and way of life (107)." Through vocation, God works through his people seeking to restore, redeem, and reconcile broken creation. God's people are his hands and feet, sent as representatives to participate in his mission in the world. Because of Christ's unconditional love and acceptance, individuals are led to share their lives, including their gifts and talents, with the hope to make a difference in the world through their labors. The idea of vocation is accessible to all of God's people, as Whelchel articulates, "Discovering our vocation is possible because it is based on giftedness, interests, passions, and human need, which are all easy to identify."[166] Church leaders should make it a priority for all congregants to discover their gifts and talents, leading them to greater calling clarity.

Faith Integration

It is important not to lose sight of the higher calling to follow Christ and to reflect his image in one's vocation, which offers a great opportunity to live incarnationally. Becky Towne described this opportunity during a doctoral lecture as "unifying the sacred and secular areas of life while showing forth God's presence."[167] She added that individuals become "the habitation of the Holy, a tabernacle, where they learn through daily activity to function in cooperation with and in dependence upon God."[168] Church is not a place to which believers go on Sunday. Believers are the temple

---

166. Whelchel, *How Then Should We Work*, 78, Kindle.
167. Becky Towne, CS 850 "Christian Spirituality," class lecture, Houston Graduate School of Theology, January 2015.
168. Ibid.

of the Holy Spirit and they take God's presence with them the other six days of the week. Through vocation, believers are "actively participating in God's purposes in the world."[169] God is calling the church to begin to integrate their faith into all areas of life, not just in those compartments designated as religious. The workplace is where most Americans spend a significant portion of every day and week, year in and year out. Seeing the workplace as a mission field to fulfill God's purposes in the world could be transformative. With a renewed view of work and a renewed sense of purpose, it is possible that a one may stop fixating on the clock, waiting for it to hit 5:00 pm.

THE WHOLE PEOPLE OF GOD

One of the customary questions to ask a fellow believer in conversation outside of the church context is, "What church do you go to?" The response is usually a specific church name and location, along with details on the pastor's name and background, and even the size of the congregation and denominational affiliation may be shared. Church members will say their church is Baptist, Pentecostal, Presbyterian, Lutheran, or so on, but the church was never intended to be reduced only to these details. The church is the whole people of God, where the Holy Spirit takes residence and empowers the lives of believers.

I felt the divisive effect of denominations at a time when I was looking for employment as a pastor. More important than character and abilities to perform the duties of the position was my denominational affiliation. If I was not a Baptist, Lutheran, or any other denomination they represented, I was automatically not considered. Yet, the church is the living body of disciples of Christ, organized with different parts like noses, eyes, arms, and ears; it should not be reduced to denominational affiliations. While I'm aware that this is a fixed reality in today's church, and a prime example of the deeply entrenched attractional mindset, the lost ideal can still be lamented and possibly regained in part. The Holy Spirit connects

---

169. Glen G. Scorgie, *A Little Guide to Christian Spirituality: The Three Dimension of Life with God* (Grand Rapids: Zondervan, 2009), 139.

the people of God to one another, giving them a common Savior and task in the world. Each member has a function to work collaboratively for the sake of equipping and extending the Kingdom, regardless of the institutions one represents.

Building His Kingdom

In her spirituality class Houston Graduate School of Theology, Becky Towne stated, "We each have a calling upon our lives to participate in the purposes of God, to play a role in his grand designs." In addition to the corporate calling of the whole church, the body of Christ has members with individual callings. With this perspective, the whole people of God should be clergy in their homes, neighborhoods, and workplaces. When there is a clear demarcation between the clergy and laity, the parts represented in Christ's body are significantly reduced. Towne further broke down the roles of all believers into three areas: "Taking care of creation, restoring people to God through Christ, and participating with Jesus in the building of his kingdom." The whole body of Christ is comprised of many parts, and when it encourages and fosters individual callings, the whole can function to its full potential since its members are carrying out their parts in the world.

The Vision of *Shalom*

God's presence now rests in the church through the Holy Spirit. In this sense, the church participates with God in bringing the biblical vision of *shalom* into reality. This Hebrew word is more than trying to get people to heaven when they die; rather, it entails a comprehensive view of salvation where God is seeking to redeem the multi-faceted brokenness in the world through the church. Miller describes this holistic view of salvation as addressing the "profound moral, spiritual, social, economic, and political crises facing much of the world."[170] All members of the church body should see themselves as agents of *shalom* in their context, especially in their lines of work. In the workplace, the church thus can give testimony

---

170. Miller, *Life Work*, 653, Kindle.

to the greatness and purposes of God through individual gifts, education, experience, and callings. The workplace can be transformed into a mission field where Christian workers play their part and dedicate their labors to God's vision for the world.

MEANING AND PURPOSE

The reward for leaders who gain the skills necessary in guiding their flock in finding meaning and purpose in their lives is that they can revolutionize their churches. This point is significant considering that most congregants hold regular jobs, including stay-at-home moms. At the Bible Institute where I taught, several students believed that the aim of furthering their theological education was eventually to leave their current positions in secular society and go into full-time ministry working in a church. There is a prevailing expectation that graduating from a Bible college should lead to a full-time ministry position where graduates will be able to devote all their time to the "work of the Lord." The church does its part by giving seats of honor at events and conferences to such credentialed clergy, creating a culture that all people should be aspiring to these positions of prestige.

Because the credentialing process is expected, students enter with every expectation of the appropriate rewards. Though it is possible that some may fill full-time ministry positions, the reality is that most students will not have this opportunity and will have to continue in their current work settings. For some, nothing will change after they graduate, only the way they begin to see their work setting, which should be as a mission field. For many working in the public domain, their mindset is "do their eight and hit the gate," so 5:00 pm becomes the most important part of the day when they can finally clock out. Once the work day is over, they exit their work settings as fast as possible so they can go home and do what they enjoy and feel passionate about. Viewing their current contexts as a mission field will give employees greater purpose in their workplace. With purpose in mind, the church will not be looking to leave their workplaces but will see this environment as an opportunity to be incarnational in the public domain.

Thrive Where Planted

According to Scorgie, "The vocational dynamic of Christian spirituality addresses the problem of meaninglessness in life."[171] One's vocation can offer purpose, a reason for existing, and a sense that life matters. Conversely, a lack of clarity regarding one's calling can lead to frustration and disgruntlement when individuals end up in careers that do not bring fulfillment. Individuals make unwise career choices because they lack the essential tools needed to find clarity. Without a sense of purpose, life can seem meaningless without a reason to be alive. Additionally, individuals are not able to represent Christ in a worthy manner when a job or career does not bring joy. The result of fostering a missional focus in people's lives could lead to a renewed sense of purpose in the workplace.

Individuals then can wake up in the morning excited about the day, sensing a special responsibility and task to which to devote their lives. It is difficult for individuals to be "salt and light" in the workplace when the experience is reduced to a paycheck. It is a challenge to sustain a good attitude when Christian workers do not have a sense of meaning in their labor. When individuals feel a sense of calling in their daily lives, however, they are better able to thrive in their positions, knowing that they are participating in something bigger than themselves. As churches and Bible colleges implement missional ideas into their congregations, vocational discernment will be an important aspect in developing workplace missionaries. Church leaders must be intentional in equipping the laity to seek missional purpose for their lives, seeking to cultivate an atmosphere that helps them discover ways to be part of God's Kingdom plan in the workplace.

Job and Career

It is important to differentiate between the terms "job," "career," and "calling." A job is a means to a paycheck so one can pay the bills for the month. A job is something people must do unless they want to be delinquent on their bills. Jobs usually come and go and many see each one as a

---

171. . Scorgie, *A Little Guide to Christian Spirituality*, 111.

stepping stone to something better down the road. If another job comes around that pays better, workers will gladly move on to the next company. Often, a job can be a "freedom taker" from the activities and tasks to which people want to devote their lives. Often, the skills and talents required to perform the tasks at a job can be accomplished by anyone. The training and hiring of employees is highly automated, and is designed this way because the turnover is usually high. Such employees do not require any sort of expertise, but companies just need warm bodies to perform the job descriptions. College and high school students will get a job but the intention is not long-term. It is simply to get them through to the next phase of life without burdening their parents for money all the time. Even older adults often have to settle for a job to earn extra spending. For others, a job is transitory while completing academic studies. Unfortunately, many get stuck in dead-end jobs with no real upward mobility, but they must stick it out to fulfill financial responsibilities.

A career is a step up from a job. It is more stable and long-term, and workers seeking a career have the 3 Ps in mind: pay, promotion, and prestige. Individuals seeking a career are often motivated by an increase in pay and moving up the corporate ladder. Employees who are in a career track have spent thousands of dollars acquiring specializations needed to work in chosen fields. The hope is that, through dedication and hard work, they can move up in the company and attain notoriety within the ranks. Usually, if someone switches companies, he or she will pursue a career with another company in the same field. Employers motivate their employees by offering certain bonuses at the end of the year and other related benefits. The more one works in this field, the greater marketability they attain as they acquire competence and experience.

Unlike a job that does not have clear direction, a career follows a sequence of jobs in a field. A career path aligns with an individual's education and experience. If a person graduates with a bachelor degree in Business Administration, the expectation is that he or she will follow this or a related career track for life. This seems to be the trend in America, especially in a highly specialized culture where employees need a degree, certification, or license for just about any field in the marketplace. Those who speak a second language and desire to be a translator at a hospital, for example, are required to attend a school that is accredited for training translators to take the entrance exam, the passing of which will ensure qualification as a Certified Medical Interpreter. Even then, many hospitals require additional hands-on experience before applicants are considered for employment, so being bilingual and certified is not enough to be hired as an interpreter.

High school and college students see a career as the next step in life while a job is only a stepping stone. Public schools prepare high school students for college or trade schools by showing them salary comparisons from different careers prevalent in the marketplace. This creates a culture in which the main concern for pursuing a career is the financial compensation. Encouraging students to pursue their calling is rarely discussed, even though it might better align with their gifts, passions, and priorities in life. These students, more than likely, will pursue an education at a university or trade school with financial gain as the pinnacle of importance. People need to make a living, but when money is the primary motivator, it can be a distraction to the plans and purposes of God in their lives. The wrong aspiration has led many to career dissatisfaction. In contrast, when people pursue their calling, the passion and commitment that goes with it will lead them to accomplish extraordinary tasks for the right reasons.

Pursue Calling

It is possible to have a job or career without a sense of calling to the work being performed. For this reason, being intentional about pursuing a calling is important for God's people. The church could make a tremendous impact in the process of helping the laity discern their callings. When individuals recognize the amount of time that will be spent at the workplace during their life span, it should encourage them to pursue their calling. The life span, from birth to about 14 years of age, is considered the early or pre-adolescent years. From 14 to 18, individuals are in high school. From 18 to 22, they pursue further education in a trade school or university. Then from 22 to 72, those who stay healthy could spend 50 years of their lives in the workplace. The ability to work into one's seventies will depend greatly on an individual's health and financial situation. Employees, who find fulfillment and purpose in the workplace, have a greater reason to stay healthy. From 73 on, most will be retired, spending this final phase attempting to enjoy their remaining years. Since the bulk of people's lives will be spent at the workplace, it would make much more sense and give people's lives greater purpose if they would pursue their calling, rather than only a job or career.

When individuals pursue their calling, it gives them a sense of destiny. They were created by God to fulfill a special task in the world, which goes much further than just earning a paycheck, seeking a promotion, or climbing the corporate ladder. It is a source of joy to be involved in work when people feel they are contributing to the expansion of the Kingdom. It gives individuals a sense that they were born to complete a special assignment in the world given to them by God. When individuals feel that they were appointed to fulfill this purpose, it compels them to reach their full potential in life because they dedicate their whole being to this duty. This calling is what individuals feel they were born to do, and it aligns with who they are and what they were created to accomplish in life.

JOURNEYING WITH OTHERS

When writing about essential leadership tasks, Callahan stated that supporting others in finding their "specific mission in the world" will bring meaning and purpose to their lives. I know this to be true, because I spent three years of my life intentionally seeking answers to the question, "Why am I here on this earth?" This led me to a journey of self-discovery, when I attained much needed clarity and a greater sense of direction for the future. This experience allowed me to compile the best tools and sources available, which, in turn, led to developing a course to help others achieve greater clarity like I had. After combing through multiple resources and reading extensively on calling, I formulated the "Five Purpose Pillars," which are discussed in more detail below. Three years of exploration in personal discovery, vocational discernment, personality assessments, and theology of work studies led to the development of a coaching course.

Some of the questions to which the coaching responds are, "What am I good at?" "What career or calling should I pursue?" or "Is there a plan for my life?" The course helps students gain greater self-awareness in five critical areas: Primary gifts, passions, personality, priorities, and purpose. After students complete these sections, the discoveries they make along the way allow them to write well-thought-out mission and vision statements. With increased clarity and direction, they can make informed decisions with increased self-awareness. This section is not intended to guide readers in discerning their mission in life but only to provide a brief overview of key concepts involved in discerning one's calling. Following are the five purpose pillars that guide students in creating a clearer picture for their future.

FIVE PURPOSE PILLARS

1. **Primary Gifts**: This pillar seeks to answer the question, "What am I good at?" This pillar is comprised of three areas: Natural, acquired, and spiritual gifts.
    a. *Natural gifts*: These are talents with which individuals are born and that come naturally, although they must learn to develop them fully. People tend to gravitate toward these roles because of their natural capacity to carry them out. They gain fulfillment using these gifts because they can perform at a higher level while exerting less effort and energy. These gifts allow individuals to work smarter, not harder, but they still need to exercise and practice to gain mastery. John Holland's Hexagon (Figure 2) is a tool used for assessing natural gifts.
    b. *Acquired gifts*: These are earned in life through hard work and commitment. Individuals gain skills and capacities that build up over time, which include life achievements and overcoming challenges. To attain these gifts, goals are set and attained. A handout for acquired gifts is also helpful in

building a résumé, which includes areas of education, experience, excellent, and extra-curricular activities.

c. *Spiritual gifts*: These gifts cannot be earned but are given supernaturally to enable one to engage in God's mission. They are utilized to help and assist in healing and restoring the brokenness in our world, surpassing human capabilities. They are a gift of grace for the benefit of others. They are meant to be used in collaboration with people who have different spiritual gifts, as no one person can accomplish the work of Christ in our world.

Figure 2. John Holland's Hexagon

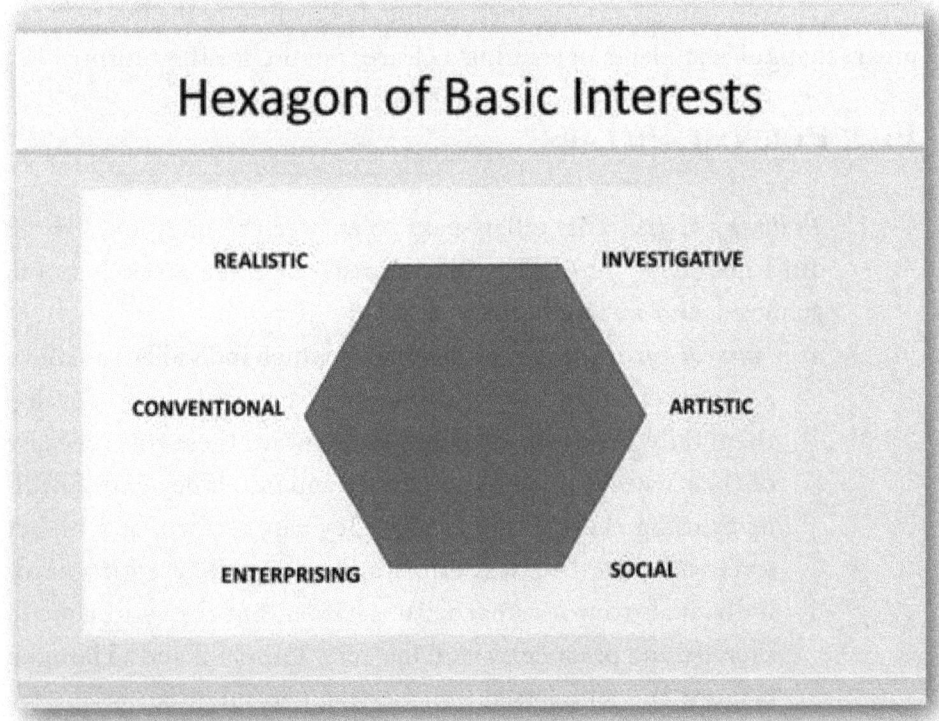

2. ***Passions***: God gives individuals a heart to serve in certain areas, during the exercise of which they are energized and filled with life. These areas bring excitement when performed, and individuals

find themselves talking about them consistently. Some people would work in this area for the rest of their lives if they could make a living doing it. These areas allow people never to work another day, because it is what they enjoy doing so is no longer work. Instead, it is an interest that keeps coming to mind, keeping individuals up late at night and rising early in the morning.

3. ***Personality***: A variety of preferences make up a person's personality, which, when discovered, will help individuals decide where they are best suited to work, play, and serve. People's work environment should provide a good fit so they can be who they are. Different work environments are best suited for different types of personalities. The Myer's Briggs Personality test is a good source to comprehend possible work environments.

4. ***Priorities***: It is important to establish guidelines and principles that will guide individuals in making their best decisions. A list of six priorities should serve as a guide in making decisions that align with one's beliefs, convictions, and values. These principles say a lot about what is important to a person and can define character. They should be well thought out and responses tend to reveal where individuals are on their journeys. Priorities can be adapted to an individual's current situation.

5. ***Purpose***: To attain direction in life, it is helpful to articulate personal "mission" and "vision" statements. A mission statement defines what individuals are supposed to be doing with their lives, while a vision statement gives them a picture of where they want to be in the future, setting a goal or dream to look forward to in the future. Mission and vision statements can provide great sources of motivation to do one's best.

It is also important to create an action plan. This timeline can help individuals identify, visualize, order, and prioritize the steps they need to take to fulfill their lifegoals. After they can articulate the mission and vision statements, they should list the goals they need to achieve in six months, one year, three to five years, and ten years that would draw them closer to their purpose. This action plan serves as a guide; allowing individuals to remain flexible since changes might arise that may require adjustments to be made. Individuals should avoid being rigid when developing a plan and be open to unexpected opportunities or changes. The next few pages present examples of mission and vision statements for some of the students I taught at the Bible Institute. Notice the significant differences between pre-course and post-course responses. The names have been changed for confidentiality.

Table 2. Post-Course Follow-up Responses

Participant	Pre-Course	Post-Course
1. Adrian Melendez Age: 32 Occupation: A/C Tech	The calling of God in my life is not clear; I only feel that it will be a leadership role. It has been said to me that God is placing a pastor's heart in me. My main concern is to follow his call whatever that may be.	**Mission:** I want to be a pastor in my workplace by utilizing my technical abilities and my gifts of hospitality and mercy so I can spread the gospel. I serve best in an environment that allows me to serve others by representing Jesus through my abilities and actions. It is important that I do this because of the love I have for Jesus. I will achieve this purpose by continuing my studies and influence in my workplace. **Vision:** In ten years, my business success will cause me to be influential and I will be able to fund multiple church plants around the world.

2. Jenny Romero Age: 29 Occupation: Homemaker	God is calling me to serve and work with him and for him in a specific ministerial and spiritual capacity.	**Mission:** I want to be a civil rights spokesperson advocating for abused women and children by utilizing my social, communication, and encouraging abilities, so I can share with others God's love and justice. I serve best in an environment that allows me to be sociable, harmonious, and where I can freely express myself. It is important that I find this because I will be helping families experience personal growth and healing. I will achieve this by using my experience in suffering and partnering up with a women's and children's center. **Vision:** I want to provide a home or shelter to women and children of abuse where they can be restored emotionally and spiritually.

3. Jose Cepeda Age: 28 Occupation: Manufacturer	My calling is still not clear but I have been preaching and I am passionate about it. In reality, what is important to God are souls of human beings that have eternity in hell or heaven. This is why it is important to preach the word and take it seriously because preaching is not a game, and it is something that requires dedication and commitment.	**Mission:** My desire is to be a preacher by utilizing my social abilities, my knowledge and helps gifts, which will make a better preacher. I serve best in an environment where I can preach the word freely. It is important that I find this because it is very important to me to speak about God's love. I will achieve this goal by continuing to study God's word. This will lead me to make an impact in the Kingdom of God because I will be attracting souls for God. **Vision:** I would like to share the real gospel of God and show the world that there is a God who loves souls and hates sin.

4. Roger Ontivarez Age: 25 Occupation: Construction	I am called to be a teacher so I can encourage youth in the learning of his word. Also, serving God on the worship team is an area I really enjoy because worship creates the atmosphere.	**Mission**: My desire is to become an engineer in structural design utilizing my abilities to resolve logical problems and design expertise. I serve best in an environment that allows me to work freely using my professionalism and creativity. It is important that I pursue this path so I can be competitive and successful in the workforce. I will achieve this calling by disciplining myself to completing basic and superior studies. This will take me to make an impact in the Kingdom of God because I will be interacting with a variety of people, from my supervisors to some employees I may be managing. **Vision**: One day I hope to found an organization that builds houses in third world countries.

5. Diego Benitez Age: 20 Occupation: Computer repair	I am called to be sensitive to God's voice, whether he wants me to keep studying or if he wants me to be more involved in ministry.	**Mission:** My desire is to become a music producer utilizing my enterprising, artistic, and prophetic abilities so I can transmit a message on behalf of God. I serve best in an environment which allows me to have integrity, speak truth, and develop my creativity. I will reach this goal by continuing to serve in my church and learning about the Scriptures. **Vision:** I hope that in 2-3 years I will be able to produce my own CD.

6. Eduardo Salgado Age: 25 Occupation: Maintenance	I am called to be a teacher in Sunday School, but the classes would be more academic, going deeper into the word, in comparison to a preaching or devotional.	**Mission:** I want to be an accounting officer and use my administrative, bookkeeping, and counseling abilities so I can practice good stewardship of God's finances. I serve best in an environment where I have access to financial tools and programs to do the job. I need to develop in my professional competency by continuing to study English, gain experience at my current job, and get my G.E.D. **Vision:** I want to be a certified public accountant in ten years.

7. Maria Ramos Age: 22 Occupation: Hair Stylist	The calling of God for my life is of worship. He has given me a spirit of availability and of worship. He has also given me gifts for music. When I gave my life to Christ, being on the worship ministry was the first thing God called me to do. To him be the glory!	**Mission:** I want to become a healthcare worker by utilizing my social, giving, and helping abilities so I can see others healed and receive equal healthcare. I serve best in an environment where I can be the hands and feet of Jesus. It is important that I do this because I want equal healthcare. I will achieve [my goals] by furthering my studies. **Vision:** I hope to be a missionary healthcare worker in Africa.

| 8. **Javier Herman** Age: 18 Occupation: None | Well, I do not really know; I haven't found out yet. This is how I feel but this is just me. I feel like I am not called to be a pastor or to be a missionary. I am not sure what God has planned for me, but I am sure it will be something that will fit me. | (Did not articulate a mission statement) |

| 9. **Luis Cordova** Age: 42 Occupation: General Contractor | The calling I have felt from God is evangelism and [to] plant a church. I want to learn to worship God with all my heart and strength. | **Mission:** My desire is become a pastor by utilizing my gifts of evangelism, faith, and healing so I can bring restoration and salvation. I serve best in an environment where I can serve and see lives changed. I will achieve this goal by growing in self-confidence and biblical preparation. This will allow me to fulfill the mandate that God asks from me. **Vision:** In ten years, I will have established a church in Guatemala after returning. |

CONCLUSION

Leaders should serve as conduits in helping others pursue and discover their callings. The church should function as a type of spiritual service station where God's people are renewed, refilled, equipped, and sent with the empowering of the Spirit to participate in God's mission in the world. The concept of vocation is inclusive, allowing ordinary believers to see themselves as missionaries and ministers in their communities as they serve their neighbors in daily tasks. The love and grace extending to God's children leads them to share their lives, including their gifts and talents, with the hope to make a difference in the world through their labors. Vocation in this context offers purpose, a reason for existence, and a sense that life matters, especially in the marketplace.

Whelchel writes, "The work we do in the here and now is important to God and serves as a signpost to point others to the New City, the City of God, where all of God's children will live one day in perfect shalom."[172] Lester DeKoster believes that "churches have disconnected discipleship form everyday life."[173] He recognizes the need to reformulate the meaning of work, adding, "The largest portion of life, our work in the home and in our jobs, is excluded from our concept of discipleship and stewardship."[174] Church leaders must foster a whole-life discipleship culture in their churches, helping members to integrate the various compartments of life by equipping them with the tools to be successful missionaries in their workplaces and communities.

BIBLICAL INSIGHTS ON CALLING/VOCATION

In Ex. 3:10, the Lord called Moses from a burning bush and commanded him by saying, "Now go, for I am sending you to Pharaoh. You must lead my people Israel out of Egypt." Moses had a special call on his life that came directly from the voice of God. Lewis reflects on how the mission of God became Moses's mission requiring "a life dedication to being part

---

172. Whelchel, *How Then Should We Work*, 95, Kindle.
173. Lester DeKoster, *Work the Meaning of Your Life* (Grand Rapids: Christian's Library Press, 1982), 63, Kindle.
174. Ibid.

of God's plan for creation and liberation."¹⁷⁵ This same voice is calling individuals today to a special assignment where they can join God in his redemptive plan. When Christians can see their work in this way, there is less likelihood that they will experience it as a curse or drudgery.

In the Old Testament, there are different strands of the Hebrew verb *qara*, but there is one meaning pertinent to this chapter appearing approximately one hundred times, which means "to call, invite, or summons," and which applies "particularly with reference to God calling upon his people, corporately and individually, to follow him in trust and obedience."¹⁷⁶ A good example of this use of the verb is in God's call or summons to Samuel, "Then the LORD came and stood and called as at other times, 'Samuel! Samuel!' And Samuel said, 'Speak, for Thy servant is listening'" (1 Sam. 3:10, NAS). The boy Samuel finally discerned the call after the Lord attempted to get his attention several times. Similarly, there are multiple call narratives in the Old Testament that "emphasize a divine encounter and commission"¹⁷⁷ to fulfill a mission or task (e.g., Abraham, Gen. 12:1-9; Moses, Ex. 3:1-21; Isaiah, Isa. 6:1-8). In addition to individual calls, God summons entire communities. When he called "Israel to be a kingdom of priests" (Ex. 19:6), David Noel Freedman affirms that it means "the larger Israelite community in exile receives a commission to be God's servant" (Isa. 49:3-6).¹⁷⁸

In the New Testament, the Greek verb *kaleó* can mean "to call, summon or invite," which is similar in the Hebrew; for example, in the Gospels, Jesus "calls" people to repentance (Mt. 9:13; Mk. 2:17; Lk. 5:32) but also to follow him as disciples (Mk. 1:20, 2:17).¹⁷⁹ The New Testament also contains call stories where there is "an invitation to relationship with God as well as a summons to a specific function or mission"¹⁸⁰ (e.g., Paul:

---

175. Lewis, *Choosing Your Career*, 38.
176. Renn, ed., *Expository Dictionary of Bible Words*, 160.
177. William H. Myers, "Call, Calling, Call Stories," in *The New Interpreter's Dictionary of the Bible, A-C*, vol. 1 (Nashville: Abingdon Press, 2009), 529.
178. David Noel Freedman, *Eerdmans Dictionary of the Bible* (Grand Rapids: Eerdmans, 2000), 211.
179. Renn, ed., *Expository Dictionary of Bible Words*, 161.
180. Myers, "Call, Calling, Call Stories," 529.

Acts 9, 22, 26; the Twelve: Mk. 1:14-20, 2:13-14; Mt. 4:18-22; Jn. 1:43-51). Whether "the call" is made to individuals or people, there is an invite to "a life of faith in Christ and his regeneration of their hearts that enables them to follow that summons," as Ryken, et al, write, who also note that there is a general call to all people to a "life of faith and obedience" and "to specific roles and tasks."[181]

The etymology comes from the Latin *vocare*, meaning "to call,"[182] and the Latin *vocatio*, also meaning "call," which corresponds to the Greek *kaleó*, "to call."[183] To avoid dichotomizing the clergy and laity, vocation no longer was to be thought of as an exclusive call to ordained ministry. Scorgie describes how every believer now is called to be "actively participating in God's purposes in the world," adding that God calls his people to carry out his purposes and plans for humanity in "a particular line of work and way of life."[184] Through various callings, whether teacher, policeman, or mechanic, God works among his people, seeking to restore, redeem, and reconcile broken creation, by reweaving *shalom* through their vocations.

WORDS AND PHRASES TO REMEMBER

Vocation/Calling: The work that God's people can dedicate their lives to and join him in fulfilling his plans and purposes in the world.

Shalom: A biblical vision for the world from the Hebrew word translated "peace" in English, which entails a comprehensive view of salvation. God is seeking to bring this vision to fruition by redeeming the multi-faceted brokenness in the world through the church, which includes the profound moral, spiritual, social, economic, and political crises in the world.

---

181. Ryken, Wilhoit, and Longman, eds., "Calling, Vocation," *Dictionary of Biblical Imagery*, 133.
182. Scorgie, *A Little Guide to Christian Spirituality*, 107, Kindle.
183. Xavier Leon-Dufour, *Dictionary of the New Testament* (San Francisco: Harper and Row, 1980), 422.
184. Scorgie, *A Little Guide to Christian Spirituality*, 139, Kindle.

SCRIPTURES TO REFLECT

Gen. 12:1-9
Ex. 3:10
1 Sam. 3:10
Jn. 4:34

DISCOVERY QUESTIONS

1. What are two ways the church has erroneously categorized full-time ministry as a step above or more spiritual than work in the public sphere?

2. What are two ways you can begin to seek greater purpose and meaning in the workplace?

3. Why is it important that leaders begin to equip the church with the tools to pursue their callings/vocations?

4. What are two changes that could possibly occur in someone's life when they begin to see their work as a mission field or as a calling?

Last Things

Pushed to the Fringes

> I wanted to let you know that we have a written policy to not have anything related to personal views attached to our email signatures, especially messages that are going out to our customers. Please make sure your email signature only contains your contact information and/or the company's information and remove any reference to the Bible.

THE ABOVE EMAIL MESSAGE WAS sent to one of my students at the Bible Institute by her supervisor at work. She shared this message with the class as we discussed the challenges of evangelism in the workplace. These conflicts between employees expressing their faith and company policies are becoming increasingly common in America's workplaces. There has been "a significant loss of the traditional and expected status, respect, influence, and even power"[185] toward Christianity in today's post-Christendom reality. As I was driving on the freeway during the Christmas season, I could not help but notice a gigantic billboard with a picture of Santa Claus that said, "Go ahead, skip church. Just be good for goodness sake!" This billboard was sponsored by American Atheists in protest of the holiday and the custom of going to church during the Christmas season. It should now be expected that protests like this, but perhaps with even stronger mes-

---

185. Terry Coy, *Return to the Margins: Understanding and Adapting as a Church to Post-Christian America* (Abbotsford, WI: Aneko Press, 2015), 142, Kindle.

sages, will become commonplace instead of isolated incidents. Christians should not be surprised or caught off guard as society continues to reject their faith affiliation.

CHRISTMAS TIME IS HERE

Another illustration of the growing secularity in society came from a newspaper article that showed increased religious tensions in the public domain. Christmas time has been a season where Christians have expressed their faith with little resistance or challenge. Until recently, the general population has been accepting of the Christmas traditions that are embedded in the culture and have become a way to celebrate the season, even for nonbelievers or nominal Christians. Now the season has become a time of increased holiday litigation where secular groups have attempted to ban manger scenes from courthouses and companies have forbidden their employees to say "Merry Christmas," but instead to use the religion free "Happy Holidays." With increased tensions, Christian leaders have been ill-equipped to navigate the change in the temperature in American society toward Christianity.

The Yale Humanist Community began an initiative called the Green Light Project that has sought to "join them by creating something festive and inspiring that celebrates the season in a secular way."[186] This group planned to commission an artist to craft an art display that would celebrate "hope and the human spirit in a non-religious way"[187] at the New Haven Green. The goal was to create a public art piece to complement other religious displays so the non-religious population could be represented. This open challenge has produced intense emotional reactions from Christian leaders whose response has been to become angry and defensive and find ways to oppose and fight against these movements. Acting as if the church still yields power and prominence in society, these leaders assume that their political and judicial representatives will side with them.

These types of conflicts have been on the rise and there is no sign of slowing for equal representation in the public square. Some public

---
186. Tom Krattenmaker, "Waging Peace on Christmas," *USA Today* (Dec. 18, 2015), 7A.
187. Ibid.

officials have leaned toward a neutral posture and have decided to ban all expressions, religious and non-religious, so as not to entangle themselves in the feuds. On one occasion, a judge ordered the removal of a nativity scene from the Baxter County courthouse in Oklahoma when a group filed a lawsuit against its public presence. Then, when a non-religious group advocated to place a "Happy Winter Solstice" banner in the same courthouse, they also were told no. These examples are signs of the times and how groups are challenging the established Christmas religious expressions in the public arena. As the nation becomes increasingly secular, Christians should expect more confrontations, and they should prepare to navigate the hostile seas as the church moves to the margins.

Increasing Trend

Marginalization of the church is a trend that is likely to increase in all realms of society, including schools, businesses, government, and hospitals. Doctors, teachers, and public servants are finding it more and more difficult to be open about their faith. Companies are setting policies restricting their employees from sharing their faith to avoid any clashes at the workplace with co-workers or customers. American society has created a culture of religious sensitivity where the best policy is to "leave your beliefs at home" to avoid any unnecessary confrontations. This new reality can potentially form nominal Christians who respond by practicing their faith and spiritual duties only where it is socially acceptable, usually during a scheduled worship service or Bible study. Christians are forced to put on a different value system throughout the week to find acceptance and to assimilate into a secularized culture, causing them to live fragmented lives. When Christianity essentially was the state-endorsed religion in America, as it had been for most of its history, believers could be open about their faith because it was assumed that most of the nation was Christian. Then, it was the non-Christians who felt ostracized by society, but the tide is beginning to change. Today, Christians who step out in faith and are open about their beliefs in the public domain can expect opposition.

Post-Christendom, postmodern American society is increasingly unchurched and Christians are being forced to adapt to an environment that is becoming increasingly pagan. The secularization of America makes living as a Christian more difficult than it has ever been. Christians no longer are guaranteed acceptance by society and cannot depend on the unwavering support from the state that they had in the past. On the contrary, Christians are increasingly on the receiving end of persecution in varying degrees of intensity, with some examples more blatant than others. Isolating itself from mainstream culture and huddling in a spiritual bubble, however, is not the answer; instead, it will render the church powerless and ineffective.

Growing Secularity

The "propping up" of Christianity above all other religions by the state is seen less and less. Even though this separation was made long ago at the inception of the Constitution, the founding fathers did not intend to promote secularization. In the U.S., the separation between church and state, originally designed to protect the church from the state, now has been inverted and the two entities continue to grow distant and distinct from each other. Today, with the plurality of religions, the state's responsibility is to be religiously neutral, ensuring that the interests of all minorities are protected and none exercises undue influence over the other. This legal claim has caused the influence of the church to be moved even further to the margins. Unfortunately, some Christian groups continue to operate from the center instead of the margins, mindlessly repeating a centuries old paradigm that had strayed far from its New Testament roots. Resisting this entrenched model, missional leaders operating with a marginalized mindset must arise if they are to impact society. No longer can the church function in an attractional posture in a post-church era operating from the comfort and security of their established institutions. Instead, more fluid and organic forms of church need to emerge.

Post-Church Culture

The term post-church or post-Christian is used by scholars in contemporary America to describe the trend of an increasingly churchless society, particularly among the disaffected, younger, postmodern demographic.

Research conducted by the Barna Group, in *You Lost Me: Why Young Christians Are Leaving the Church*, shows that seventy-five percent of Americans between the ages of eighteen and twenty-nine consider themselves "spiritual but not religious." The authors also reported that nearly three out of every five young Christians disconnect permanently or for an extended period of time from church life after age fifteen.[188] Given these numbers, if this trend continues, America soon will look more like secular-saturated Europe. Some scholars also use the term "post-Christendom" for the new, marginalized state in which the church finds itself today. The church in increasingly losing its voice and influence in the public sphere. For this reason, the church needs to adopt a marginalized mindset in a new era where they are pushed further to the fringes.

LIKE AN OUTSIDER

The first-century Christians lived on the fringes of Roman-dominated, Jewish society where they were true outsiders and had to learn to trust God in an environment that was neither accepting nor friendly. The primitive church directly attributed any increase the church experienced to the work of the Holy Spirit. In this context, none of the growth was due to the church's prominence and popularity, yet it grew rapidly and spread around the world. As modern society transitions deeper into a post-church culture, the church will feel increasingly like an outsider, even in the spheres of society where it had once felt like an insider. Murray argues that Christians today should function as "aliens, exiles, and pilgrims in a culture where we no longer feel at home."[189] Christians no longer feel at home in a post-Christian era and feel more like resident aliens living in a land that is not their own, seeking acceptance and refuge from an unaccommodating society.

The Bible is filled with images of God's people living as foreigners and aliens in a country that was not their own. In both the Old Testament and New Testament, "The image of the foreigner, stranger, sojourner or

---

188. The Barna Group, "Six Reasons Why Young People Are Leaving the Church," September 28, 2011, accessed April 1, 2015, https://www.barna.com/research/six-reasons-young-christians-leave-church/.
189. Murray, *Post Christendom*, 20.

alien is a major biblical archetype."[190] Rah describes an alien as someone who is "unable to relate to the host culture. In fact, one way of interpreting 'alien' would be as an immigrant."[191] The feeling of living on the margins of society without the inherent rights of citizens is a recurring theme that the church should adopt given the circumstances in a post-Christian culture. It is an historical theme of God's people, who do not live at home but rather on the fringes of society; vulnerable, unwelcomed, and uncomfortable, yet attempting to live faithfully to their calling.

The Church Is Losing Influence

As the church in America loses more of its authority and influence, it is more essential than ever for the laity to learn to function as local missionaries in a pluralistic, technologically savvy, and multicultural context. The church is moving further away from the center of society, no longer as influential as it was during Christendom. Scholars are beginning to face this fact: "Christianity in North America has moved (or been moving) away from its position of dominance as it has experienced the loss not only of numbers but of power and influence in society."[192] The church continues to lose ground in the public sectors of society. The voice of the church is no longer seen as authoritative as it once was. Therefore, the church should adapt to their fringe status and not think as if something strange is occurring. Post-Christendom is here to stay, and the church predictably will continue to be pushed ever further to the margins. Rather than living in shock or denial, the church instead should begin living incarnationally as representatives and signs of the Kingdom within society.

From the Center to the Margins

As the influence of the church continues to move from the center to the margins, American society, particularly the younger generation, continues

---

190. Ryken, Wilhoit, and Longman, eds., *Dictionary of Biblical Imagery*, s.v. "Foreigner," 300.
191. Soong-Chan Rah, *Many Colors, Cultural Intelligence for a Changing Church* (Chicago: Moody, 2010), 869, Kindle.
192. Guder, ed., *Missional Church*, 1.

to grow unchurched. Yet, there are patterns, practices, and traditions that are a way of functioning as if the church still holds considerable influence and prominence in the public arena. There are growing pockets in society where Christians are encountering greater resistance and pressure to keep beliefs separate as they engage in the public domain. To remain relevant, the church needs to develop an outward, centrifugal posture recognizing it no longer wields the influence it once had when it was clearly at the center of society. The church can no longer expect outsiders on their own initiative to seek out its services and activities. This was the expectation during a time when America was considered primarily a Christian nation. With the streams of changes like globalization, pluralism, and secularity happening in American society, the church could greatly benefit from missional training.

A Missional Framework

Even though Christendom has passed, there are still churches that hold a posture characteristic of that bygone era. The ideology of church leaders in Christendom tends to favor hierarchal, centralized, and inflexible patterns of leadership. This is in stark contrast to organic, egalitarian, and fluid forms of leadership that are missional. Missional leadership empowers the members of the body to participate in God's mission. The gift of leadership (e.g., Rom. 12:8), bestowed by the Spirit, is not to control or monopolize ministry but to empower and nourish participation from the whole community. With a collaborative approach, a multiplicity of gifts is made available to the body for the sake of God's mission in the world. When the entire body of Christ is empowered, they become missionaries in the spheres where they live and work.

A primary goal of this book was to offer a framework of ministry that could assist in broadening the horizons of the members of the church, which is particularly important in an unaccommodating, post-church era. These ideas and concepts sought to provide an outward, missional mentality to guide the church in having a greater impact in surrounding communities and workplaces. Many have grown bored and tired of the traditional church routine and are looking for meaning and purpose in their day-to-day life.

Some have felt stagnant and are seeking ways to be more intentional about integrating faith and service into other realms of life beside primarily on church grounds. This book sought to get the missional "juices flowing," so the laity could begin the process of moving from a status of members to that of local missionaries. The impact the laity can have in the public domain—the hardest-to-reach places in society—will only strengthen local churches.

Closing Thoughts

The secularization of America in the public sphere is a trend that is continually gaining momentum. This is readily seen as Christ is taken out of schools and football coaches are no longer allowed to pray before games. In the public square, Christian monuments with the inscription of the Decalogue are taken down for cultural sensitivity in a pluralistic society. The examples are endless of how American culture continues to reject the notion that the church is still an authority in society. Given these difficulties, it is easy to "light a lamp and put it under a basket," but Christians are called to set their light on a "lampstand," so "it gives light to all who are in the house" (Mt. 5:15, NKJ). No longer is the church holding a position of prominence characteristic of the Christendom era; rather, it needs to operate from the fringes. The church should be viewed as a pilgrim people journeying through hostile and unwelcoming territory while seeking to be faithful to Christ. The new, marginalized status in post-Christendom will require the church to leave its religious turf and engage an unaccommodating society incarnationally.

Given the challenges in society, Christian leaders should adopt an exile mindset where they serve from a place of humility, vulnerability, and discomfort in a culture that is becoming less accepting of their faith. A megachurch in the Houston area is located right next to I-10, the busiest highway that cuts through the city. Drivers cannot help but stare at an enormous white cross projecting out of its facilities. Whether they want to or not, they are forced to look at the cross as they drive by because it is impossible to avoid. An image that was conjured in my mind as the cross stared down on me was a dad serving his kids salad and telling them, "You are going to eat it and like it!" Many are turned off by the arrogant attitude of the church forcing its beliefs into the hearts and minds of America. The general population feels less compelled to support the Christian value system even though traditionally that has been the norm.

BIBLICAL INSIGHTS

The Babylonian exile in the Old Testament shows the difficulties of living on the margins. God left the Jerusalem Temple with his people and dwelled with Israel in a strange and pagan land far away from their home. In this land, they were clearly a minority. Virtually all the locals served multiple gods but not Yahweh. Away from their home and temple, they were forced to adapt to their new reality. Israel had "to find new ways of practicing their customs and religious faith in a climate that was often less accommodating of what the local population would have determined to be strange practices,"[193] writes Beach. When in exile, God's people were vulnerable with few rights, living as foreigners and resident aliens in a land not their own. They had to learn how to stay faithful to Yahweh while living as model citizens for fear of their oppressors. Israel was deported to Babylon against their will and had no alternative but to learn to assimilate into a strange land. They learned to trust in Yahweh even when it was difficult to do so considering their extreme circumstances.

The New Testament also has images of God's people not feeling at home and living in a strange land. In the Gospels, Beach describes Jesus as "a model of exile insofar as he is depicted as one who is away from his true home (Jn. 1:1-14; Phil. 2:3-8)."[194] This exile status was also adopted by the first-century church as they fled their home country due to Roman persecution. In a state of desperation and seeking a better life, they were considered outsiders in a land ruled by the Roman Empire. Despite their marginalized status, the Lord had a purpose and plan for them. As Beach puts it, "Through the exile, God would use Israel redemptively."[195] Rah

---

193. Beach, *The Church in Exile*, 713, Kindle.
194. Ibid., 1528, Kindle.
195. Ibid., 845, Kindle.

describes the cultural mandate found in Scripture as a call to "engage rather than categorically reject the surrounding culture."[196] When living on the fringes, the choice of staying isolated from the surrounding culture is tempting and provides the easiest alternative since engaging culture brings discomfort and rejection. Yet, Christians are called to be "salt" and 'light" amid culture, even when it is difficult to do so. Seeking to be faithful to Christ within culture and not isolated from it is the way Christians can be witnesses and give glory to God through word and deed in their daily interactions.

In the New Testament, the Greek noun *paroikos* appears "four times meaning 'stranger,' 'foreigner,' or 'sojourner' (Acts 7:6, 29; Eph. 2:19; 1 Pt. 2:11)," an experience that encompasses all believers in the New Testament who "live their lives as strangers on this earth while they journey toward their true home in heaven."[197] In the book of Hebrews, believers are described as "strangers and exiles on earth" and seeking "a better country, that is, a heavenly one" (Heb. 11:13, 16, RSV).[198] For first-century Christians, the hope was that one day they would finally find a home where they could experience rest in the promised "new heaven and new earth" described in the book of Revelation. The church found itself in the "already, but not yet," experiencing glimpses of the Kingdom ushered in by Jesus Christ, but not yet realized fully until his second coming when he would restore all things once and for all. Meanwhile, the church was not to be isolated and passive from its current reality, since, until this time, the church was not fully at home. From the epistle of Peter, Beach interprets how the church was to live in this in between state:

> The language of the epistle does not speak of salvation as escape or abandonment of this life; instead, Peter's focus is on the promises that God offers for the future. Peter wants his audience to understand that what is to come in the future now casts its shadow

---

196. Rah, *Many Colors*, 284, Kindle.
197. Rah, *Many Colors*, 301, Kindle.
198. Ibid., 251.

backward, affecting life and work of the church in the present and thus offering a way of shaping its current identity. The fact that what we do now has an impact on what will come in the eschatological future inspires faithfulness (1 Pet. 1:9) and joy in the midst of the current challenges the church faces (1 Pet. 1:6, 8).[199]

WORDS AND PHRASES TO REMEMBER

Christendom: An American popularized term copied from the European version, in which societal culture placed churches and Christianity clearly at the center of public life. At the center of society, the church attempted to influence policy, morals, and institutions from a position of influence. Some churches still operate from powerful traditions, attitudes, and patterns that stem from a time when the church was relevant and central to public life.

Post-Christendom: The current trend in America where the church is increasingly losing influence and prominence in society, particularly among the younger generation. The increasingly unchurched society is resembling the secularization of society that has happened in many European nations.

Secular: Attitudes, activities, and behaviors that do not seek to align or abide by a set of religious or spiritual principles or rule. The public sectors in America are increasingly becoming secular and devoid of intentionally following any biblical direction.

SCRIPTURES TO REFLECT

Acts 7:6, 29
1 Pet. 2:11
Heb. 11:13,16

---

199. Beach, *The Church in Exile*, 3190, Kindle.

DISCOVERY QUESTIONS

1. Give an example of how you have felt marginalized and living as a stranger because of your Christian faith.

2. Give two examples where you have seen an increased secularization in your context, especially in the public domain.

3. Name a group considered marginalized from whose story Christians can learn how to navigate the treacherous waters of post-Christendom.

BIBLIOGRAPHY

Alexander, T. Desmond, and David W. Baker, eds. *Dictionary of the Old Testament Pentateuch*. Downers Grove: InterVarsity, 2003.

Allen, Scott D. *Beyond the Sacred-Secular Divide: A Call to Wholistic Life and Ministry*. Seattle, WA: YWAM, 2011.

Arias, Mortimer. *Announcing the Reign of God: Evangelization and the Subversive Memory of Jesus*. Eugene, OR: Wipf & Stock, 1984.

Badcock, Gary. *The Way of Life: A Theology of Christian Vocation*. Eugene, OR: Wipf and Stock, 2002.

Beach, Lee. *The Church in Exile: Living in Hope After Christendom*. Downers Grove: InterVarsity Press, 2015. Kindle.

Beale, Gregory K. "Eden, the Temple, and the Church's Mission in the New Creation." *JETS* 48/1 (March 2005): 5-31. Accessed April 2, 2015, *ATLA Religion Database with ATLASerials*, EBSCO*host*.

Boadt, Lawrence. *Reading the Old Testament: An Introduction*. New York: Paulist Press, 1984.

Bosch, David J. *Transforming Mission: Paradigm Shifts in Theology of Mission*. Maryknoll, NY: Orbis, 1991.

Brueggemann, Walter. *Living Toward a Vision*. Philadelphia: United Church Press, 1982.

Bureau of Labor Statistics. "American Time Use Survey" (2013). Accessed March 20, 2015, http://www.bls.gov/tus/charts/home.htm#work.

Burnett-Bletsch, Rhonda. *Studying the Old Testament, A Companion.* Nashville: Abingdon Press, 2007.

Callahan, Kennon L. *Effective Church Leadership: Building on the Twelve Keys.* San Francisco: Jossey-Bass, 1990.

Coy, Terry. *Return to the Margins: Understanding and Adapting as a Church to Post- Christian America.* Abbotsford, WI: Aneko Press, 2015.

Dekoster, Lester. *Work: The Meaning of Your Life: A Christian Perspective.* Grand Rapids: Christian's Library Press, 2010. Kindle.

DeSilva, David A. *An Introduction to the New Testament: Contexts, Methods & Ministry Formation.* Downers Grove: InterVarsity Press, 2004.

Evans, Craig A., and Stanley E. Porter. *Dictionary of New Testament Background: A Compendium of Contemporary Biblical Scholarship.* Downers Grove: Intervarsity Press, 2000.

Freedman, David Noel, ed. *Eerdmans Dictionary of the Bible.* Grand Rapids: Eerdmans, 2000.

Frost, Michael. *Exiles: Living Missionally in a Post-Christian Culture.* Peabody, MA: Hendrickson, 2006.

———. *The Road to Missional: Journey to the Center of the Church.* Grand Rapids, MI: Baker Books, 2011.

———, and Alan Hirsch. *The Shaping of Things to Come: Innovation and Mission for the 21st-Century Church.* Peabody, MA: Hendrickson, 2003.

Gibbs, Eddie. *Church Morph: How Megatrends are Reshaping Christian Communities.* Grand Rapids, Baker Academic, 2009.

Gibbs, Eddie, and Ryan K. Bolger. *Emerging Churches: Creating Christian Community in Postmodern Cultures.* Grand Rapids: Baker Academic, 2005.

Gonzalez, Justo L. *The Story of Christianity: The Early Church to the Present Day.* Peabody, MA: Prince Press, 1985.

Green, Joel, Scot McKnight, and I. Howard Marshall. *Dictionary of Jesus and the Gospels.* Downers Grove: InterVarsity, 1992.

Guder, Darrell L., ed. *Missional Church: A Vision for the Sending of the Church in North America.* Grand Rapids: Eerdmans, 1998.

Guinness, Os. *The Call: Finding and Fulfilling the Central Purpose of Your Life.* Nashville: Thomas Nelson, 2003.

Herrington, Jim, R. Robert Creech, and Trisha Taylor. *The Leader's Journey: Accepting the Call to Personal and Congregational Transformation.* San Francisco: Jossey-Bass, 2003.

Herrington, Jim, Steve Capper, and Trisha Taylor. "The Faithwalking Complete Notebook." Accessed February 21, 2013, http://www.missionhouston.org/documents/MH%20files/FWCompleteNotebook.pdf.

Hirsch, Alan. *The Forgotten Ways: Reactivating the Missional Church.* Grand Rapids: Brazos Press, 2006.

Hubbard, David A., and Glenn W. Barker, eds. *Word Biblical Commentary Series.* Dallas: Word Books, 1993.

Kennard, Douglas W. *A Critical Realist's Theological Method.* Eugene, OR: Wipf and Stock, 2012.

Kennedy, John W. "Redefining Sacred Space." *PE News*, May 26, 2015, Accessed May 30, 2015, http://penews.org/Article/Redefining-Sacred-Space/#sthash.hO80OvHK.dpuf.

Kinnamann, David, and Aly Hawkins. *You Lost Me: Why Young Christians are Leaving the Church*. Grand Rapids: Baker Books, 2011.

Kise, Jane, David Stark, Sandra Krebs Hirsch. *Life Keys: Discover Who You Are*. Bloomington, MN: Bethany House, 2005.

Koeshall, Anita and John. "Ecclesiology-To-Go: Images of a Missiological Ecclesiology." Lectures presented at Assemblies of God Theological Seminary (Fall 2010). J. Philip Hogan World Missions Series Monograph, vol. V, 15.

Lewis, Roy. *Choosing Your Career, Finding Your Vocation: A Step-by Step Guide for Adults and Counselors*. New York: Paulist Press, 1989.

Leon-Dufour, Xavier. *Dictionary of the New Testament*. San Francisco: Harper and Row, 1980.

Liebe, Sarah. *Medical Student's Handbook for Electives in Global Health: Insights from a Fellow Traveler* (2011). March 30, 2015, http://www.usd.edu/~/media/files/medicine/scholarship-pathways/spp-sarah-liebe.ashx?la=en.

Luther, Martin. *Luther's Works*, vol. 44. Edited by Jaroslav Pelikan and Helmut T. Lehmann. Philadelphia: Fortress Press, 1955, 1996.

Maller, Allen S. "Solomon: the Too Wise King." *Jewish Bible Quarterly* 39, no. 2 (2011): 91-94. Accessed April 2, 2015, *ATLA Religion Database with ATLASerials*, EBSCO*host*.

Mancini, Will. *Church Unique: How to Cast Vision, Capture Culture, and Create Movement.* San Francisco: Jossey-Bass, 2008.

McKnight, Scot. *The King Jesus Gospel: The Original Good News Revisited.* Grand Rapids: Zondervan, 2011.

McNeal, Reggie. *Missional Communities: The Rise of the Post-Congregational Church.* San Francisco: Jossey-Bass, 2011.

———. *Missional Renaissance: Changing the Scorecard for the Church.* San Francisco: Jossey-Bass, 2009.

Miller, Darrow L. *Life Work: A Biblical Theology for What We Do Every Day.* Seattle, WA: YWAM Publishing, 2009. Kindle.

Murray, Stuart. *Post Christendom: Church and Mission in a Strange World.* Waynesboro, GA: Paternoster, 2004.

Myers, Allan C., ed., *The Eerdmans Bible Dictionary.* Grand Rapids: Eerdmans, 1987.

Niebuhr, Richard H. *Christ & Culture.* San Francisco: HarperCollins Publishers, 1951.

Newbigin, Lesslie. *The Open Secret: An Introduction to the Theology of Mission*, rev. ed. Grand Rapids: Eerdmans, 1995.

Placher, William C., ed. *Callings: Twenty Centuries of Christian Wisdom on Vocation.* Grand Rapids: Eerdmans, 2005.

Rah, Soong-Chan, *Many Colors: Cultural Intelligence for a Changing Church.* Chicago: Moody, 2010. Kindle.

———. *The Next Evangelicalism: Freeing the Church from Western Cultural Captivity*. Downers Grove: Intervarsity, 2009. Kindle.

Renn, Stephen D., ed. *Expository Dictionary of Bible Words*. Peabody, MA: Hendrickson, 2005.

Roxburgh, Alan J. *Missional Map-Making: Skills for Leading in Times of Transition*. San Francisco: Jossey-Bass, 2010.

——— and M. Scott Boren. *Introducing the Missional Church: What It Is, Why It Matters, How to Become One*. Grand Rapids: Baker, 2009.

——— and Fred Romanuck. *The Missional Leader: Equipping Your Church to Reach a Changing World*. San Francisco: Jossey-Bass, 2006.

Ryken, Leland, James C. Wilhoit, and Tremper Longman III, eds. *Dictionary of Biblical Imagery*. Downers Grove: Intervarsity Press, 1998.

Sakenfeld, Katharine Doob, ed. *The New Interpreter's Dictionary of the Bible*, vols. 1-5. Nashvillle: Abingdon Press, 2006.

Scorgie, Glen G. *A Little Guide to Christian Spirituality: The Three Dimension of Life with God*. Grand Rapids: Zondervan, 2009. Kindle.

Sills, Michael. *The Missionary Call: Find Your Place in God's Plan for the World*. Chicago: Moody Publishers, 2008. Kindle.

Snyder, Howard A. *Models of the Kingdom*. Nashville: Abingdon Press, 1991.

———. *The Problem with Wine Skins: Church Structure in a Technological Age*. Downers Grove: InterVarsity, 1977.

Stark, Rodney. *For the Glory of God*. Princeton: Princeton University Press, 2003.

Steinke, Peter L. *Congregational Leadership in Anxious Times: Being Calm and Courageous No Matter What*. Lanham, MD: Rowman and Littlefield, 2006.

Stevens, R. Paul. *The Other Six Days: Vocation, Work, and Ministry in Biblical Perspective*. Grand Rapids: Eerdmans, 1999. Kindle.

Stone, Bryan P. *Evangelism after Christendom, The Theology and Practice of Christian Witness*. Grand Rapids: Brazos Press, 2007. Kindle.

Strong, James. *The Strongest Strong's Exhaustive Concordance of the Bible*. Grand Rapids: Zondervan, 2001.

Thomas, W. H. Griffith. "Is the New Testament Minister a Priest?" *Bibliotheca Sacra* 136, no. 541 (1979): 65-73. Accessed June 25, 2015, *ATLA Religion Database with ATLASerials*, EBSCO*host*.

Tyra, Gary. *A Missional Orthodoxy: Theology and Ministry in a Post-Christian Context*. Downers Grove: InterVarsity Press, 2013.

Unger, Merrill F., and William White, Jr., eds. *Nelson's Expository Dictionary of the Old Testament*. Nashville: Thomas Nelson, 1980.

Van Gelder, Craig, ed. *The Missional Church and Leadership Formation: Helping Congregations Develop Leadership Capacity*. Grand Rapids: Eerdmans, 2009.

———, Dwight J. Zscheile, and Alan Roxburgh. *The Missional Church in Perspective: Mapping Trends and Shaping the Conversation*. Grand Rapids: Baker Academics, 2011.

Ward, Peter. *Liquid Church: A Bold Vision to be God's People in Worship and Mission – A Flexible, Fluid Way of Being Church*. Peabody, MA: Hendrickson, 47.

Whelchel, Hugh. *How Then Should We Work? Rediscovering the Biblical Doctrine of Work*. Bloomington, IN: Westbow Press, 2012. Kindle.

Wingren, Gustaf. *Luther on Vocation*. Translated by Carl C. Rasmussen. Eugene, OR: Wipf and Stock, 1957.

Wright, Christopher J. H. *The Mission of God: Unlocking the Bible's Grand Narrative*. Downers Grove: InterVarsity, 2006.

Wright, Walter C. *Relational Leadership: A Biblical Model for Influence and Service*. Colorado Springs: Biblica, 2000.

Yoder, John Howard. *For the Nations: Essays Public and Evangelical*. Grand Rapids: Eerdmans, 1997.

www.ingramcontent.com/pod-product-compliance
Lightning Source LLC
LaVergne TN
LVHW041249080426
835510LV00009B/655